Tales of Old Oxfordshire

Tales of
Old Oxfordshire

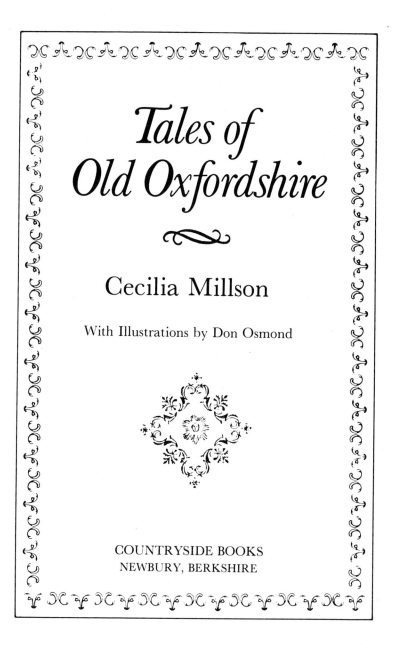

Cecilia Millson

With Illustrations by Don Osmond

COUNTRYSIDE BOOKS
NEWBURY, BERKSHIRE

First Published 1983
©Cecilia Millson 1983

COUNTRYSIDE BOOKS
3 CATHERINE ROAD
NEWBURY, BERKSHIRE

ISBN0 905392 20 5

Designed by Mon Mohan

Printed in England by J.W. Arrowsmith Ltd., Bristol.
Typeset by Cambrian Typesetters, Aldershot

To Timothy, Richard and Simon.

Contents

1.	Banbury's Cross	11
2.	The Battle of Chalgrove Field	14
3.	Morris Dancing	17
4.	Romance at Bablockhythe	22
5.	The Maharajah's Well	25
6.	Elizabethan Scandal	32
7.	Tragedy in the Hayfield	37
8.	The Meadows of Yarnton	40
9.	The Rollright Stones	45
10.	Empress Matilda's Escape	48
11.	The Levellers at Burford	51
12.	May Day and Christmas Customs	54
13.	Fair Rosamund	59
14.	The Profligate Earl	62
15.	Disaster on Christmas Eve	67
16.	Where Goes the Garter?	71
17.	Love Poisoned	74
18.	The Lovells of Minster	79
19.	Blankets from Witney	82
20.	A Lucky Escape	86

21.   Tales of the Highway   89

22.   Binsey's Treacle Well   92

OXFORDSHIRE — The map overleaf is by John Speede and
shows the county as it was in the early Seventeenth Century.

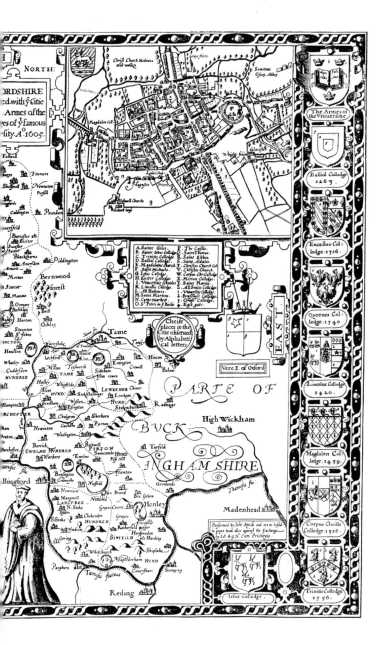

NORTH:

...ORDSHIRE
...d with ẙ Citie
...Armes of the
...res of ẙ famous
...sity. A°. 1605.

Christ Church Meadowes
and walke

Stone friers

Sometimes Osney Abbey

Magdalen Col:

Wright friers

Gloester

Augustine friers

Hollwell Church

Holliwell briog

EAST.

PARTE OF

BVCK
INGHAMSHIRE

High Wickham

Turfild

Grenland

Thamesis flu.

Madenhead

Henley

Reding

Chiefe places in the citie obserued by Alphabeticall letters.

A. Sainte Giles.
B. Sainte Iohn Colledge.
C. Trinitie Colledge.
D. Ballioll Colledge.
E. Magdalane Church.
F. Saint Michaels.
G. Lyllies Colledge.
H. Exceter Colledge.
I. Vniuersitie Schooles.
K. Lincolne Colledge.
L. All Hallowes.
M. Saint Martins.
N. Corne Market.
O. S: Peters in ẙ Baili.

P. The Castle.
Q. Saint Thomas.
R. Saint Ebbes.
S. Saint Aldates.
T. Christes Church Col:
V. Christes Church.
W. Corpus Chri Colledge.
X. Merton Colledge.
Y. Saint Maries.
Z. Vniuersitie Colledge.
1. All Soules Colledge.
2. Brasenose Colledge.
3. Oriall Colledge.
4. Egit gate.

Vere. E. of Oxford.

Performed by John Speede and are to be sould in popes head alley against the Exchange by I.S. & G.H. Cum Priuilegio.

Iesus Colledge.

The Armes of the Vniuersitie

Balliol Colledge 1263

Exceter Col: ledge. 1316.

Queenes Col: ledge. 1340

Lincolne Colledge 1420.

Magdalen Col: ledge. 1459.

Corpus Christi Colledge 1516.

Trinitie Colledge 1556.

Banbury's Cross

Ride a cock horse to Banbury Cross,
To see a fine lady upon a white horse,
With rings on her fingers and bells on her toes,
She shall have music wherever she goes.

To anyone who has known and loved that nursery rhyme in childhood the first sight of Banbury Cross, standing firmly at the town's principal crossroads, brings an exclamation of delight, even if those who are more familiar with the famous landmark, and the traffic problems which it causes, are less enthusiastic as they sit beneath its shadows and wait impatiently to resume an urgent journey.

The present cross is of the Victorian era and there is some doubt as to whether it stands on the actual site of Banbury's nursery rhyme cross. The town was the proud possessor of three crosses in mediæval days, the white cross on the outskirts of the town, the market cross, and the bread cross which, it is thought, was connected with the distribution of an annual bread dole.

At the beginning of the seventeenth century only one cross remained and this was speedily disposed of by a zealous mob of Puritans who destroyed it so thoroughly in 1602 that hardly a stone was left standing. The Archbishop of Canterbury ordered its re-construction but this order was apparently ignored by a town noted for its Puritanical adherence, and for the next two and a half centuries Banbury had no cross standing in the town. Even the exact locations of the three mediæval crosses became confused. Banbury Cross was but a name.

11

The origin of the fine lady is also obscure. Indeed, she figures as an *old* lady in some versions of the rhyme but the more dashing and romantic fine lady is the prime favourite, at least, with the children. But who was the intrepid horse-woman, old or young?

A lady of the Fiennes family from nearby Broughton Castle, whose elegant riding habit would have won the admiration of bystanders as she rode through Banbury, has been suggested as a possible contender for the title. But the more popular theory gives the leader of the annual May Day procession pride of place in the controversy. How attractive she would have looked as she sat on her prancing white horse, dressed in her May Day finery, with bells jingling as she rode towards the town cross where all important matters were proclaimed and discussed. Perhaps she dismounted at the steps to preside over the celebrations in which boys on their more humble cock or hobby horses would follow the Hobby Horse man engulfed in his decorated frame?

If May Day celebrations are at the centre of the rhyme's origin then it is understandable that a veil was drawn over the memories of the happy day, for the Puritans of Banbury were among the first to denounce the May Day revels as idolatrous, and the celebrations disappeared as surely and completely as the offending cross.

But tradition dies hard. Although some of the versions of the rhyme that passed from word of mouth to printed page in the eighteenth century did not mention the fine lady, eventually she triumphed, and rode straight into the pages of the children's books, never to be displaced. Only one difficulty remained. There was no cross in a town that was now famed for this particular monument.

The Victorian residents therefore decided that the erection of a new cross would be the very thing with which to pay tribute to a royal occasion; the forthcoming marriage of Princess Victoria, the eldest child of Queen Victoria, to Prince Frederick William of Prussia.

The wedding took place on 25th January, 1858, but the

townspeople of Banbury were not to be hurried. They considered most carefully the merits and possible authenticity of
several sites, and the plans for the monument. At length a
position at the cross roads by the Horse Fair, the place of one
of Banbury's ancient markets, was selected, and a design by
Mr. J. Gibbs of Oxford was accepted for the cross.

This design was based on that of the Eleanor crosses erected
by Edward I at the end of the thirteenth century to mark the
resting places of his beloved queen's coffin as it was taken
from Lincoln to Westminster for interment. Hardly, it seems,
a suitable choice for a monument to mark the commencement
of the newly weds' life together, but no-one seems to have
objected on that score and by April, 1859, fifteen months after
the event it was to commemorate, work commenced on the
new Banbury Cross. By October of the same year it was
finished, complete with the town's arms and statues of
Banbury's most famous sons, but for some reason three panels
remained empty. In 1911, to mark the coronation of King
George V, it was decided to add the statues of three
sovereigns, Queen Victoria, King Edward VII, and King
George V. The vacant places were duly filled and the cross
was finally complete by 1914.

Time, however, does not stand still, and before another
decade had passed doubts were being expressed as to the
wisdom of having a large cross standing at the centre of a busy
road junction. But a proposal to move the monument brought
protests from far and wide, for the nursery rhyme was loved
not only in England but far beyond our shores and so the
proposition was abandoned or, at least, shelved indefinitely.
Modern traffic still rumbles uneasily around Banbury Cross
and bows before the old tradition of the fine lady riding
proudly on her pure white horse.

The Battle of Chalgrove Field

There was a feeling of anxiety in the villages of eastern Oxfordshire during the month of June, 1643. Both Royalist and Puritan families shared the possibility of being actively involved in the Civil War, for they were surrounded by the opposing forces of King and Parliament.

The Earl of Essex occupied Thame and his Parliamentary troops were spread out around a wide area of the countryside. King Charles I had his headquarters at Oxford and it was from there that Prince Rupert rode out at the head of 1,700 men.

The Prince had been informed that a convoy had left London for Thame carrying £21,000 to the Earl, and he was determined to capture the prize. He passed through Tetsworth and Potscombe on his way to Chinnor where he learned that a force of newly recruited Parliamentary soldiers were billeted in the village. His soldiers fell upon the unfortunate men, killing fifty who attempted to escape and rounding up the remaining one hundred and twenty as prisoners. All too late, Prince Rupert realised his mistake. The attack had raised the alarm and alerted the neighbourhood. The convoy was warned of the Prince's whereabouts and made for the cover of the Chiltern Hills. The Royalists dared not follow as they knew they would be ambushed as soon as they entered the densely wooded slopes.

A disappointed and frustrated Prince Rupert turned his men towards Oxford, skirmishing as he went and after directing his infantry to Chiselhampton Bridge to protect his retreat, he made his way to Chalgrove where Parliamentary supporters were massing in answer to a call to arms. One who had responded to the call was Colonel John Hampden the celebrated Member of Parliament and staunch opponent of the King, who was staying at Watlington. He joined a group of Parliamentarians and rode to Chalgrove field where he assumed command of the forces.

The Puritans knew that they had little chance of defeating their more numerous and better equipped opponents but they bravely hoped to hold the Royalists until reinforcements joined them in the battle. Prince Rupert was informed of their plan by one of his spies and described it as sheer insolence. He led the charge towards the hedgerows which sheltered the Parliamentarians and bore down upon them. They stood their ground as long as possible, fighting with great courage, but they were no match for the Prince's superior forces and as their line of resistance broke they fled from the battlefield.

The Prince did not attempt to follow them. He knew that Essex would soon bring reinforcements and thought it wiser to return to Oxford. He did not know at that time that John Hampden had been present. In fact, the Colonel had been badly wounded in the shoulder and had been forced to leave the battle early, hanging over his horse's neck. He tried to reach Pyrton, a village he knew well for it had been the home of his first wife Elizabeth Symeon, but Royalist troops barred the way so he turned towards Haseley and made his way painfully to Thame. He reached the shelter of the Greyhound Inn but died six days later and was taken for burial to his own village of Great Hampden in Buckinghamshire.

John Hampden was sincerely mourned in Thame both by the townspeople and his Parliamentary friends. He had attended the Thame Grammar School, founded by Lord William of Thame in 1575, where he had been a boarder for nine years. His friends knew that they had lost a good counsellor, a man of integrity and a loyal patriot, for all he did he sincerely believed was in the best interests of his country.

He is mainly remembered for his opposition to Ship Money, an ancient tax once levied in time of war upon ports and maritime towns and counties to provide ships for the King's service. King Charles I not only revived the tax but levied it in inland counties as well, whereupon John Hampden refused to pay the amount levied on his property in Buckinghamshire. It was not so much the tax that offended him but the fact that the King had acted without the consent of Parliament. Chiefly due to Hampden's spirited resistance the tax was finally declared illegal by statute in 1641.

Today an obelisk stands on Chalgrove Field. Erected by Lord Nugent and his friends during the nineteenth century, it not only commemorates the battle but bears an inscription which records the merits of John Hampden. It concludes:

> Within a few paces of this
> spot he received the wound
> of which he died while
> fighting in defence of the
> free monarchy
> and ancient liberties of England.
> June 18th. 1643.
> In the two hundredth year
> from that day
> This stone was raised
> In reverence to his memory.

Morris Dancing

Morris Dancers have become a familiar sight at country shows and fêtes in recent years and a crowd quickly gathers to see the white clad figures dance into the arena attended by their musicians, and, quite frequently, by a fool, or a giant hobby horse.

The Cotswolds have been a centre for Morris dancing for centuries and their own special variety of the traditional dance, called the Cotswold Morris, has six dancers in its team, and a musician and a fool. Four traditional Cotswold Morris teams survive in Oxfordshire at Abingdon, Bampton-in-the-Bush, Chipping Camden and Headington Quarry.

Quite how or when it all began no-one knows. Traditionally Morris Dancing has its roots in the pagan fertility rites in which young men stamped upon the earth in the hope of making it yield a good harvest. Their identity was hidden beneath a surfeit of streamers and their faces were blackened, a custom which was later associated with the word Morisco (Moorish) and so, it is thought, the name of Morris was evolved. The sword which is still carried by some teams is a symbol of the sacrificial rites which were part of the ancient ceremony.

Whatever its origin, Morris dancing became a popular mediæval and Tudor pastime, and James I gave it his blessing in his *Book of Sports* as it was one of the sports and pastimes which he thought suitable for Sundays and Holydays after the end of Divine Service.

Together with other amusements Morris dancing received a serious setback during the years of Oliver Cromwell when such frivolities were banned but evidently the old dances were

not forgotten. The first May Day after the restoration to the throne of Charles II saw a giant maypole erected in the Strand, and Samuel Pepys recorded that as soon as the pole was in position the Morris men appeared waving their scarves and dancing to 'the ancient Musick'.

The instruments used to make this music are the pipe and tabor, the fiddle and the concertina (the first two are better known in Oxfordshire as the whittle and dub) and nowadays the accordion is also permitted. The tunes and dances are traditional but every village developed its own slightly different version of the dances, and these bear the name of the village to which they belong.

That many of these dances are remembered today, when they might easily have been forgotten in a changing rural

18

life-style, is due to a strange coincidence which took place one Boxing morning in 1899.

By this time Morris dancing had become associated with Whitsuntide and many teams practised for weeks for their one public appearance on Whit Monday, but in 1899 times were hard and men of the Headington Quarry team were unemployed. The idea came to them that a dance on Boxing Day would not come amiss, and onlookers might be willing to drop a few coins into the collecting box during the season of goodwill.

As the men set off down the village street they were watched by a Christmas visitor, a music master by the name of Cecil Sharp, as he stood by the window in his host's drawing room. He was so fascinated that he went out to talk to the dancers and fell into conversation with William Kimber. It was the beginning of a lifelong friendship, and the great work of Cecil Sharp who travelled all over England to find and record the traditional dances and songs. The Folk Dance Society, formed in 1911, ensured that forgotten dances would be revived and remembered in future years.

In the small Oxfordshire town of Bampton-in-the-Bush no revival was necessary for it claims an unbroken record of six hundred years of Morris dancing. As in other country places the twentieth century brought its problems — the drift of young men to large industrial towns — two world wars — at times it was not easy to find the men to dance but William 'Jinky' Wells worked unceasingly, playing the fiddle, dancing the steps, teaching the youngsters, just as he had been taught by his grandfather in his own boyhood. He was the Bampton dancers' guide and inspiration and had the satisfaction of knowing that he had succeeded in keeping the team together when he died in November, 1953, at the age of eighty five years.

The present Squire (or President) of the Bampton Traditional Morris Dancers, Francis Shergold, proudly showed me the silver sword and cake container which is inscribed:

In Memory of
William Wells
1868 — 1953
The Gift of the Morris Ring
to the
Bampton Morris Dancers.

(The Morris Ring is a federation of all the Morris Clubs in England)

When the Bampton team go into the streets on Whit Monday (now Spring Bank Holiday) the sword is decorated with flowers, one of which must be a peony, and the container, which fits over the sword is filled with pieces of fruit cake. These are distributed to the bystanders to bring them luck.

The dancers assemble at nine o'clock in the morning and soon the teams are spread through the town. They wear their club's distinctive variation of the Morris costume over the traditional white trousers and shirts — embroidered baldricks and badges, decorated black hats and, of course, bells on their legs. The bells jingle as the men jump high in the air to clash their sticks or wave their handkerchiefs. The traffic is brought to a standstill, but no-one seems to care; it is the day of the Morris dancers.

Mr. Shergold has been associated with the Bampton dancers since 1935 when as a young lad he acted as ragman, the name given to the boy who carried the men's coats as they danced through the town. He watched and learned the dances and very occasionally he was allowed to take his place in the team — a proud moment for a young ragman.

Nowadays the boys are more privileged and do not have to serve such an apprenticeship. The older dancers make way for young enthusiasts more readily, only too pleased that they are willing to learn the dances. The fool with his bladder belabours the team while it waits for any changeover of dancers to take place. Not that there is much waiting time. The energy of the dancers is fantastic. Naturally liquid refreshment is plentiful when they dance outside one of the many inns in the town, but it is richly deserved, especially when it is a hot day.

The entertainment for the crowds which gather on the pavement is almost non-stop. There is a halt for lunch and then the teams re-assemble outside the Talbot Inn for the start of the afternoon session. An invitation to dance in a shady garden is very welcome and *Polly put the Kettle on* serves as a tuneful hint as to the dancers' needs. In return the dancers bring good luck to the owners of the gardens through which they pass.

In the evening teams from other parts of England and from overseas join in with their own particular dances. Truly a great festival of dancing in a beautiful Cotswold town.

The Bampton dancers now extend their season beyond the Whitsuntide festival and dance at other times in county, national and international festivals. Their devotion to the Morris tradition should ensure that their children, and their children's children, will one day be dancing in the streets of Bampton as their forefathers have done for the past six hundred years.

Romance at Bablockhythe

∽

The stretch of the River Thames between Bablockhythe and Newbridge is the perfect setting for a love story of the mid-eighteenth century.

The pastoral scene can have changed but little since those far-off days. The cows still graze in the meadows and come down to drink at the water's edge, but the river traffic now passes in an orderly fashion through Northmoor lock whereas two hundred years ago it was forced to negotiate the troubled waters of the weirs, controlled by keepers whose cottages stood by the banks of the Thames.

One such weir, in the charge of a man named Rudge, was situated above the present lock. His daughter, Betty, was employed at the Ferryboat Inn at Bablockhythe, where ferrymen and their passengers had been served for centuries, for both ferry and inn were amongst the oldest on the river.

It was a hard, busy life for any young girl, and for one of Betty's outstanding beauty, a hazardous one as well, for some of the inn's regulars were only too ready to plague a pretty maidservant when they grew tired of watching the cudgel playing and shin kicking contests. These were rough, cruel sports, but popular pastimes in country inn yards where men would gather on Sunday mornings, or whenever work permitted, to see their favourite gamesters display their skill. The tap room would resound with stories of past contests, and cracked heads and scarred legs would be displayed with pride.

It was hardly a pleasant environment for a girl of Betty's disposition. The fact that a beautiful girl of twenty-one remained unmarried, in an age when youthful marriages were common, makes it appear likely that Betty was a quiet, shy girl who was only too thankful to turn her back on the inn and walk home along the river bank to her father's lonely cottage. Work was hard to come by in that secluded place, but perhaps she dreamed as she walked that some day her life would change and she would leave the inn for ever. If so, her daydream was to be realised beyond her wildest hopes.

One fateful day a young undergraduate from Christ Church, Oxford, came to fish at the weir. He saw Betty Rudge and became enslaved by her beauty. She, in return, must have been attracted by his quiet, studious ways for he was a man who reputedly shunned the extravagances of eighteenth century society and preferred a simple and retired life.

The undergraduate was William Flower, Viscount Ashbrook, but in spite of his noble birth he was determined to marry the humble maidservant. He sent Betty to be educated in a gentleman's household and then quietly married her, by licence, in Northmoor Church in 1766.

At first, it is said, they lived in seclusion just above Bablockhythe where the river and a small stream form an island. Here some cottages once stood, named appropriately Noah's Ark, but this was only a temporary home and they soon moved to the small village of Shellingford where their first child was born in October, 1767; a son whom they called William.

The deaths of two of their other children in infancy caused them distress in the otherwise happy years of their marriage. Unfortunately, this happiness was destined to be short lived for the Viscount died in 1780, at the early age of thirty seven. His wife must have been heartbroken, for after a moving tribute to the virtues of the Viscount, his epitaph in Shellingford Church concludes with these lines:

'He was a kind and affectionate husband, father and brother,
In him the Rich had lost a sincere and disinterested Friend,
The Poor, a compassionate and generous Benefactor.'

Betty, or Elizabeth, as she was then called, outlived her husband by twenty eight years. She died on the 23rd. February, 1808 'universally lamented in the 63rd. Year of her Age'.

The one time innkeeper's daughter surely counted herself fortunate that she had been taken from the servitude of an eighteenth century riverside inn to become the honoured wife of a kind and considerate nobleman.

The Maharajah's Well

∞

A well top in an English village is still a familiar enough sight to pass unnoticed unless it is of singular 'olde worlde' charm. One of a distinctive Eastern character immediately calls for closer inspection, and the Maharajah's well is a popular landmark in the village of Stoke Row.

The residents are justly proud of their unusual well for it was given to them by His Highness Ishree, Maharajah of Benares, one hundred and twenty years ago.

The gift came about by chance. The Indian ruler stood on a Benares hillside with Mr. Edward Anderson Reade, who was soon to become Lieutenant-Governor of the North-Western Provinces of India, around the year 1850. The Maharajah spoke of his plans to overcome the water shortage which brought such hardship to the hill dwellers. Mr. Reade remarked that he had seen similar problems in the Chiltern Hills where his father's estates spread over Ipsden and Stoke Row. He recalled that villagers depended on rainwater for their cooking and in dry seasons the precious water was passed from one cottage cooking pot to another while boys were punished for taking furtive drinks of water to quench their thirsts. Pond water was used for washing and when the water level was low washing days were indefinitely postponed. The Maharajah listened and remembered.

Over ten years passed, years which saw the Indian Mutiny, and the Maharajah wished to present a charitable gift as a token of his friendship and loyalty towards England, and, also, as an expression of his personal gratitude to Mr. Reade who had been of considerable help to him during the difficult period of the Mutiny. He decided that a well in the Chiltern Hills would be an appropriate donation.

᾿It so happened at that time that the common land in Stoke Row was being enclosed and the Commissioners were approached and agreed to give the necessary land for the installation of a public well. The Maharajah approved the site and suggested that work should commence on the wedding day of H.R.H. The Prince of Wales (afterwards King Edward VII). Consequently the 10th. March, 1863, saw the commencement of a mammoth task, the sinking of a 4ft. wide well to a depth of 368ft., or, as one report suggests, 342ft., but whatever the figure, at more than twice the height of Nelson's Column. It was a staggering feat for all the work was done by hand. The digging over, a brick wall had to be built up 30ft. from the bottom of the well. Imagine working in such an enclosed area at such a depth!

Then the pessimists declared that such a well would need a horse, or steam power, to draw up the water but Mr. Reade and Mr. Richard Wilder of Messrs. R., J., and H. Wilder of Wallingford, were not to be beaten. Between them they designed machinery so that two narrow-topped, nine gallon buckets could be wound up and down, counter balancing each other. By this method it was possible for a woman, or a young boy, to turn the handle and draw up a full bucket in ten minutes. The water then had to be baled out into the user's own containers and carried suspended from a yoke, or wheeled on a handcart to the cottage. For a fortunate few a horse drawn cart was used to transport the containers. Clean water was available at last but the effort of obtaining it still made it a precious commodity in the village homes.

The designer of the ornate superstructure was Mr. Reade himself and he answered those who criticized it by saying that *he* had designed it and was vain enough to think it could not be improved, and as it had been 'stereotyped by photography' it had better remain unchanged. His critics were silenced.

After a year's hard work the well was officially opened on Queen Victoria's birthday, May 24th. 1864.

In addition to the well a cottage was erected to house a warden. The comparative costs are interesting. £353. 13s 7d. for the well and superstructure, £39. 10s. 0d. for the machinery and a decorative elephant, and £74. 14s. 6d. for the cottage.

A condition of the Maharajah's gift was 'That the Public should have the privilege of taking water free of charge in all time to come' so that it was necessary to provide for the maintenance of the well and cottage, and to provide a small wage for the warden who lived in the cottage rent free. A happy idea was evolved.

In India a free well is maintained by the profits of a local fruit harvest, so by the further benevolence of the Maharajah four acres were purchased adjacent to the well to establish a cherry orchard; the land also provided a pleasure ground for the villagers.

A pond was constructed in the shape of a fish (a carp was part of the Maharajah's crest) and called Muchlee Pokhra; a raised mount was named Prubhoo Teela; and a shady ravine, planted with ornamental trees was known as Saya Khoond, while the place where the cherry trees grew was called Ishree Bagh.

The unusual gift was the subject of much publicity and other wealthy Indians, not to be outshone, donated gifts of wells in various parts of England, including Hyde Park and Regent's Park.

The Maharajah of Benares was pleased to remember his well whenever a royal occasion occurred. The marriage of Princess Louise to the Marquis of Lorne in 1871 prompted him to provide a new footpath to give easier access to the well, and a year later the recovery of the Prince of Wales from an attack of typhoid fever brought a gift of two hundred pounds so that the villagers could hold thanksgiving celebrations. The money was well spent.

After a suitable church service the Maharajah's dole was

distributed to one hundred and forty nine cottagers in the parish. Every household received half a pound of tea, one pound of sugar, two loaves of bread, two pounds of bacon, and a pair of good blankets marked 'Ishree'.

The gentlemen and yeomanry of the neighbourhood, thirty four in number, sat down to lunch at the Cherry Tree Inn, after which they waited upon the one hundred and fifty labourers who enjoyed a hearty lunch and plenty of good beer in a specially erected shed. The women and children had their own tea party in the schoolroom decorated with large portraits of the Maharajah and his heir.

Village sports followed and the memorable day concluded with a magnificent firework display. The highlights of the set pieces were those which blazed the Maharajah's name, 'Ishree' and the Prince of Wales' feathers in glittering colours. No wonder there were loud cheers for the donor of the feast and the Prince and Princess of Wales!

Eight years later, in 1882, an attack on the life of Queen Victoria startled the nation. In thankfulness that the wouldbe assassin had failed, the inhabitants of Stoke Row received yet another donation from their benefactor. Again a dole was given, this time of bread, tea, and sugar, and a lunch that was enjoyed at the Cherry Tree Inn; the children also celebrated with a bumper tea party. However, this treat was to be the last for many years.

In 1883 Mr. Reade retired from his long service in India. When he died in Ipsden three years later all contact was lost with Benares, but the well continued to do its good work

In 1906 main water was piped from Woodcote but the service was unreliable and the villagers still depended on the well for much of their water. An old resident told me recently that he could remember the queues which formed in 1921, an exceptionally dry year when even the well was at a very low level. In 1927 a second pipeline brought water from Nettlebed and gradually the residents of Stoke Row connected their homes to the main water supply, although a few continued to use the well as late as 1939. During the war the water was tested to make sure that it was usable in case of emergency. Even today regular tests are carried out by the Thames Valley Water Authority.

Chance started the life of the well and chance renewed the friendship between Benares and Stoke Row. In 1958 a visitor from Oxford was asked by the great grandson of the Maharajah if the well still existed. Fortunately, the visitor knew Stoke Row and was able to reply in the affirmative, whereupon contact was made between His Highness Maharajah Vibhuti Narain Singh and Mr. Michael Reade, the great grandson of Mr. Edward Reade!

The visit of H.M. Queen Elizabeth II and H.R.H. The Duke of Edinburgh to Benares in 1961 enabled the present Maharajah to once again connect the well with a royal occasion. He presented the Queen with an ivory model of the well and recalled that the centenary of the well's opening would be due in three year's time. He invited the Duke to grace those celebrations with his presence at Stoke Row so, on Wednesday, 8th. April 1964, around one thousand five hundred people waited for the arrival of the royal visitor. Mr. Michael Reade was the first to greet the Duke, and the Maharajah's representative, Mr. B. Sahi, with his wife, and fourteen year old son were also present, with an urn of water from the River Ganges flown over for the occasion.

Miss Eleanor Turner, aged eighty one, the last of the wardens, conducted the Duke to the well enclosure where Mr. J. Wilder, a great nephew of Richard Wilder, supervised the drawing of the water which was ceremoniously mixed with the water from the Ganges.

After a visit to the little cottage and participation in a commemorative church service, the Duke planted a cherry tree and met members of the Townsend family who tended the orchard.

A very special part of the day's activities followed for the Duke visited the village hall and chatted to the older residents who were enjoying a celebration luncheon. He passed from table to table and heard many stories about the well from

those who had really known its value in their younger days.

Suitable speeches and presentations took place and then, true to tradition, the Duke was taken to the Cherry Tree Inn where he lunched before leaving the village, piloting his own helicopter. Surely a day of which H.H. Ishree, Maharajah of Benares would have been tremendously proud.

Alas, hard times were to follow. After the death of Miss Turner in 1972, and the departure from the village of the Townsend family, who not only cared for the orchard and sold the cherries, but also kept the well and cottage gardens in good order, the whole property started to deteriorate. It became only too obvious that the sale of cherries from a small orchard could not produce sufficient revenue in present times for the upkeep of the well and cottage. Some other source of revenue must be provided.

It was finally decided that if the cottage, now no longer needed for a warden, could be modernised and enlarged, it could be let and so provide for the maintenance of the well, but before that scheme could be carried out money would have to be raised for the project. The discovery of severe corrosion in the well superstructure added to the worries of the trustees.

An interesting phrase had been inserted by Mr. Edward Reade in the original Trust regulations which stated that the Trustees were not to approach the successors of the Maharajah for aid as it would contravene a Hindu custom, but the present Maharajah quickly refuted this when he heard it and offered his help. Other gifts and grants followed and the residents themselves set to work to raise the necessary money with a determination worthy of the original builders of the well.

The enlargement of the cottage and the restoration of the well are already underway, and soon the hardworking money raisers of Stoke Row will have the satisfaction of seeing the Maharajah's Well, which served them so faithfully for many years, preserved for posterity.

An Elizabethan Scandal

⧰

A stone fireplace strangely set in a churchyard — but if it could only speak it might unravel a mystery which has baffled historians for over four centuries.

It is in Cumnor churchyard that the fireplace can be seen. It is set into a bank and is the only visible ruin *in situ* of the great house, Cumnor Place, which once stood there, built by an Abbot of Abingdon as a country retreat. George Owen, physician to the King, bought the property at the time of the dissolution of the monasteries but he and his family rarely occupied it and his son, William Owen, leased it to Anthony Forster, the steward of Lord Robert Dudley, a tenancy which was to bring the old house into the pages of history.

In 1550 Amy Robsart, the only daughter of a wealthy Norfolk landowner married Robert Dudley, third son of the Earl of Warwick. The Earl had been sent into Norfolk to quell a rebellion led by a tanner by the name of Jack Kett. Robert accompanied his father, and it seems possible that he met Amy during the brief period of the campaign.

Their marriage took place at the royal palace of Sheen, and was graced by the presence of the young King Edward VI. The eighteen year old country girl and her handsome bridegroom seemed destined for a happy and prosperous future, but three years later Dudley was in the Tower of London. His father, since created the Duke of Northumberland, had tried unsuccessfully to place his daughter-in-law, Lady Jane Grey, upon the throne of England when Edward

32

VI died in 1553. He paid for his failure with his life, and his sons were imprisoned, charged with conspiracy in the plot to oust Mary Tudor from her inheritance.

During the time of her husband's imprisonment Amy Dudley visited him regularly in the Tower. Later, when he and his brothers were pardoned, Robert Dudley accompanied his wife to her father's estates in Norfolk, but country life did not suit the restless, ambitious young man and he sailed to France in 1557 when war provided him with an opportunity to serve Queen Mary and so reinstate himself into influential court circles. The attainder on his family was lifted the following year and the Dudleys' possessions were restored to them.

The death of Mary on November 17th. 1558, and Elizabeth's accession to the throne found Dudley high in favour. He and Elizabeth had been friends since childhood and now the amusing, handsome courtier was in constant attendance on the Queen. He was appointed Master of the Horse, a position which covered the arrangements for the court and for all ceremonial occasions. The dashing Dudley, a fine horseman, rode beside Elizabeth and was closely watched by friends and foes alike. There were many suitors for the Queen's hand but she smiled on no-one as she smiled on Robert Dudley. There was one major stumbling block — he was a married man.

Being always at court, Dudley saw little of his wife. They had no home of their own and so Amy Dudley would stay at the houses of her husband's friends or dependants. She was always attended by servants, richly clothed, and transacted business on her lord's behalf but she felt lonely and neglected and it was rumoured in some circles that she was a sick woman. She must have felt troubled by the rumours which coupled the Queen's and Dudley's names together, and she never appeared at court herself.

After a visit to friends at Denchworth, just north of Wantage, Lady Dudley moved to Cumnor Place in 1560 to stay with Anthony Forster and his wife. Mrs. William Owen, wife of the owner of Cumnor Place, was also in residence. On Sunday, September 8th. the servants left the house to attend Abingdon Fair at Lady Dudley's instigation. When one or two demurred because it was Sunday, she insisted that they should go to the fair. When they returned from their outing, the house was in mourning. Amy Dudley had fallen down the stairs, broken her neck and was dead.

A messenger by the name of Bowes was quickly despatched to carry the news to Windsor Castle where Robert Dudley was with the Queen. By strange coincidence, Dudley had sent his cousin Sir Thomas Blount to Cumnor on Monday morning and he met the messenger on the road and was told of Lady Dudley's death. He journeyed on to Abingdon where he stayed the night, listening to local reaction to the news, before proceeding to Cumnor Place.

Lord Dudley apparently showed no sign of sorrow upon hearing of his wife's death. His concern was only for himself and the scandal the news would cause at court, for he knew only too well that his enemies would make good use of the suspicious circumstances surrounding Amy's sudden death to damage his reputation. He sent instructions to Blount to carry out full investigations, and to make sure that a jury was appointed who could be trusted to find the truth of the matter. Evidently, he did not feel it was necessary to go to Cumnor himself.

Natural causes, accident, murder, or suicide? All four verdicts were under consideration but to Robert Dudley's relief the jury returned the verdict of 'mischance or accidental death'. Lady Dudley's body was taken to Oxford where it rested at Gloucester Hall (now Worcester College) before being interred in the chancel of the Church of St. Mary the Virgin on Sunday, 22nd. September. The mourners were many but her husband was not among them.

Elizabeth's councillors, and foreign ambassadors to England, watched anxiously, for many detested Dudley and dreaded the possibility of such a man becoming the Queen's husband. Rumours were circulating that, in spite of the jury's verdict, he knew more about his wife's death than he cared to admit, and there were even whispers that the Queen knew that all was not well at Cumnor. They need not have been so anxious. Within three years the Queen had created her favourite Earl of Leicester but she still did not marry him.

Suspicion lingered on. In 1567 the circumstances surrounding Lady Dudley's death were recalled when her half-brother, John Appleyard, declared the jury had been suborned and that, in fact, she had been murdered. He was commanded to appear before the Privy Council to explain his charge but, when confronted by so imposing a body, he said that he did not hold the Earl guilty but thought it would not be too difficult to find the guilty parties, and the matter ended by his confession that he had brought the false charge out of spite against Dudley.

Meanwhile, Dudley's steward Anthony Forster bought Cumnor Place from the Owens and continued to live there until his death in 1572. There were those who believed he had been implicated in Lady Dudley's death, either on Lord Dudley's instructions or on his own account, for if his master was free to marry the Queen, his own future was assured. However, he was a man of means, married to a niece of Lord Williams of Thame, and served as Abingdon's M.P., so that his elaborate memorial in Cumnor Church seems to record the truth when it extols his virtues — virtues which make him seem an unlikely murderer.

His widow lived at Cumnor Place for the next twenty seven years, although Forster had bequeathed it to Dudley who eventually sold it to Anne Forster's cousin Sir Henry Norreys, first Baron Norreys of Ryecote.

The old house was passed down the family through the years but was never a family home again and, after a period of occupation by tenant farmers, and latterly by farm animals, the fifth Earl of Abingdon decided to use the stone of the neglected house to rebuild the church and his own house at Wytham. So in 1810 Cumnor Place was pulled down.

But according to legend the restless ghost of Amy Dudley

roamed the site of her unfortunate death. The villagers were terrified by an apparition dressed in Elizabethan costume until nine parsons came from Oxford to lay the ghost. They succeeded by drowning it in a pond near the churchyard wall, a pond which never froze again. A strange legend entwined round the secret of Cumnor Place for, despite all attempts to discover the truth, no-one has completely explained the tragedy which scandalized Elizabethan England.

Tragedy in the Hayfield

❧

John Hewet of Stanton Harcourt was a happy man as he strode towards the manor farm on the morning of July 31st.,1718. He had just requested and obtained permission to marry Sarah Drew, an eighteen year old milkmaid, whose parents were pleased to welcome a hardworking farm hand of twenty five as their future son-in-law.

The wedding was to take place the following week and John felt that he was indeed a lucky man for Sarah, dark and attractive, would make a perfect bride as she stood beside him in the parish church.

One of John's duties was to bring the herd to be milked every morning and evening thus providing the lovers with a chance to meet and make their plans for the future. No doubt there was a happy meeting that morning before they joined the other farm workers in the hayfield. They were a popular pair and everyone wished them well as they took their places and commenced work.

The day was hot and sultry and threatening clouds gathered above the haymakers. Soon, heavy rain forced them to seek shelter under the trees and hedgerows as thunder rumbled overhead and ominous streaks of lightning lit up the dark sky. Sarah, frightened, and breathless from her run across the field, flung herself down on a haycock. John raked more hay around her to provide better protection, and then lay beside her and sheltered her face with his outstretched arm as a blinding flash struck the earth.

The other workers, stunned by the ferocity of the thunder-bolt, cowed for a moment in their sheltered places, then called to one another to find if all were safe. No reassuring call came from the haycock. A wisp of smoke rose from the wet hay and the frightened men slowly approached the lovers. They gasped at what they found. John and Sarah were dead. Their bodies were unmarked save for small scorch marks on Sarah's brow and between her breasts, but they had both been killed by the fury of the storm. The following day they were buried in one grave in the country churchyard.

The sad story might well have been forgotten by the end of the century but for a poet's compassion over the fate of the rural lovers.

Alexander Pope was staying in the village as a guest of Lord Harcourt who had placed part of the old manor house (ever since known as Pope's tower) at the disposal of the poet, who needed a quiet place in which to translate the fifth volume of Homer, a work which he completed during 1718.

Pope was deeply moved by the tragedy of the storm and persuaded his host to erect a monument over the lovers' grave. He then wrote an epitaph to commemorate the event. Lord Harcourt considered that his first effort would be too difficult for country people to understand so the poet wrote a second epitaph:

'Think not by rigorous judgment seiz'd
A pair so faithful could expire,
Victims so pure Heav'n saw well pleased
And snatched them in celestial fire.
Live well and fear no sudden fate,
When God calls virtue to the grave
Alike 'tis justice soon or late,
Mercy alike to kill or save.
Virtue unmov'd can hear the call
And face the Flash that melts the Ball.'

This, too, had its critics, amongst them the Bishop of Rochester, who felt that the last line would evoke thoughts of a snowball. However, it was placed on the outside wall of the church and remains there to this day. Pope also sent an account of the story to his friend, Lady Mary Wortley Montagu. The poet was convinced that she would share his distress over the tragedy but he had misjudged the aristocratic lady who had scant time to spare for the sorrows of such humble lovers. Her reply, in verse, left Pope in no doubt as to her feelings on the matter.

'Who knows if 'twas not kindly done?
For had they seen the next year's sun
A beaten wife and cuckold swain
Had jointly curs'd the marriage chain.
Now they are happy in their doom
For Pope has wrote upon their tomb.'

Lady Mary would have been surprised to know that her own caustic verse and Pope's kindlier epitaph have contributed to a lasting memory of the unfortunate lovers.

The Meadows
of Yarnton

~~~

Holy days, feast days, and the days when ancient customs were observed, provided welcome breaks in the lives of country people of past centuries. These red-letter days were probably the only holidays they knew, for leisure time and money were both scarce and neither could be spared for long periods of recreation.

In the village of Yarnton it was on the first Monday of July that, until recently, the women used to put on their prettiest dresses, and added flowers and ribbons to their plain straw hats, before going down to the meadows. The men concentrated on the more serious business of the day.

These meadows, on the north bank of the Thames, were called Oxhay, Picksey, and West Mead. They were common land, allotted to the tenant farmers of the district who enjoyed the mowing rights. It was the drawing of lots for the fine crop of hay which these meadows yielded that made the day so exciting, both for the participants and the onlookers.

The head Meadsman was in charge of the proceedings. He thoroughly understood the complicated measuring of the lots. For the most part, the villagers were content to know that the one hundred and seventeen acres were divided into 'customary acres', that was strips that one man could mow in a day, or, as the local people so aptly described it, 'one man's mowth.' The boundaries of the strips were clearly marked by men treading up and down between them. This was called 'running the treads.'

40

The strips were originally divided between thirteen farmers, and thirteen wooden balls, about one inch in diameter and thought to be made of holly wood were used in the draw. These are in the village today and all bear names, possibly those of the original farmers, although they may have been changed over the centuries in which the balls have been used. No one knows, but the names are as follows:

Boat, White, Dunn, William, Water Molly, Green, Boulton, Rothe, Gilbert, Harry, Freeman, Walter Jeoffrey, and Parry.

The head Meadsman, and his second-in-command, proceeded to a strip in the meadow, carrying the wooden balls carefully in a bag. The crowd gathered round in expectancy and the first ball was drawn. The name was called loudly and clearly. A man, waiting with scythe in hand, stepped forward and cleared about six feet of hay from the strip. Then another man cut the initials of the claimant in the cleared ground thus preventing later argument about the ownership, although as a further precaution a clerk carefully noted the allocation.

The group then made their way to the next strip where the procedure was repeated. At last the meadows were fully allocated, including the eight acres reserved for the Vicar, and the scholars of Exeter College. These eight acres were known as Tythals or Tydals.

When the draw was finished the mowing began. This had to be completed in one day, a condition which necessitated the employment of as many as one hundred labourers from outside the village. Jugs of ale were placed along the hedgerows so that the hot, tired workers cold refresh themselves at frequent intervals, which they did with enthusiasm.

By the evening it was surprising that they could still run the races which, with a fair, ended the day's activities. The winner of the main race was presented with a garland which he placed in the church where it remained until the following year.

One wonders how many men slept on the field at night, worn out by the day's labour, the races, the pleasures of the fair, and finally the stupor induced by the strong ale.

Unfortunately trouble frequently occurred and those who were wise left the meadows by early evening. In 1815 special constables were held in readiness to deal with any disorders which might arise from the effects of too much ale. In spite of their proximity a man called Strainge was in the mood for a fight by the end of the day. A Mr. Osborne prevented him from fighting in the meadows but with an opponent named Lindsey he went across a ditch and so the combat took place in the adjoining parish of Cassington!

As the drunkenness increased and serious riots developed, respectable people were afraid to go to the meadows to enjoy the races and the fair. Matters came to a head in 1817 when a man was killed in a fight. The Vicar, the Reverend Vaughan Thomas, had been advocating for some time that three days should be allowed for the mowing instead of the customary one day. He pointed out that it would give longer employment to local people if more time was allowed, and would end the necessity of bringing in casual labourers, often the instigators of the riots. At first there was opposition to the change but eventually agreement was reached and the time was extended. The Vicar preached a sermon to his parishioners on the blessings of peace.

As the years passed there were some other changes made in the proceedings. In 1849, money was paid to the Vicar and the scholars of Exeter College instead of the tithe of hay. The number of farmers involved also decreased as farms were amalgamated or disappeared with the increasing size of the village. At last only eight farmers were left in the village. Consequently their allocation of meadow land increased but they found ready purchasers for their surplus strips if they did not need all the hay to which they were entitled.

The ceremony of allocation moved to the Grapes Inn instead of the meadows and recently the draw was ended altogether. However, the meadows are under a conservation order and will remain an area noted for lush grasses and spring flowers. The hay will still be mown, but the old ritual is no longer needed to determine the distribution of the strips to local farmers, and the wooden holly balls are kept only as a reminder of an ancient ceremony.

The Rollright Stones

It was a warm summer afternoon when I last visited the Rollright Stones, near the village of Little Rollright on the Oxfordshire/Warwickshire border. A small child slept serenely in the shade of the Stones. Her mother, the site's custodian for the afternoon, sat beside the child, busily turning her spinning wheel, and for a brief moment time seemed to stand still on the Cotswold hillside. The child stirred in her sleep. Was she dreaming of the fairies which old Will Hughes claimed he had seen over a century before as they danced round the King Stone? His wife Betty had said that she had placed a stone over the cranny into which the fairies disappeared but in the morning it was gone, and the entrance to their hiding place was clear again.

A strange story, but stories and legends surround the ancient stones as over the centuries men have striven in vain to find the true purpose behind the building of the monument. Seventy seven stones, ranging from ground level to seven feet high, stand in a circle one hundred feet wide. Storms have weathered them into grotesque shapes since they were first placed on the hillside, which is not surprising as it is thought that they date from around 1500 B.C.

To the north-east of the King's men, as the stones are called, stands the King Stone, over eight feet high, alone in solitary state. A quarter of a mile to the south east the 'Whispering Knights' lean together as though in conversation. These five stones are the remains of a Neolithic long barrow and are probably five hundred years older than the circle, but legend links them together.

The old story tells of a legendary king who was marching at the head of his army. Five of his knights stood whispering together, plotting against him, as he led his loyal soldiers forward, but when he approached the ridge above the villages of Great and Little Rollright he met a witch who claimed:

'Seven long strides thou shalt take
And if Long Compton thou can see
King of England thou shalt be'

The king strode forward, eager to reach the top of the ridge and look down upon the village of Long Compton, but as he neared his goal a mound of earth rose up before him and the old witch mocked:

'As Long Compton thou canst not see
King of England thou shalt not be.
Rise up, stick, and stand still, stone,
For King of England thou shalt be none.
Thou and thy men hoar stones shall be
And I myself an eldern tree.'

Immediately the king, his treacherous knights and all the soldiers were turned to stone to stand on the lonely hillside for ever. However, it is said that they are reprieved at times to go down into Little Rollright spinney so that they can drink from a spring. Opinions differ as to whether they go every night at midnight or only on certain holy days.

On midsummer eve in years gone by girls would go one at a time to the Whispering Knights hoping to hear a whisper about their own futures, and chippings from the King Stone were thought to bring good luck to those who held them. However, ill-luck fell upon anyone who tried to move the stones.

So, they stand today to puzzle men as to their origin and purpose. On midsummer's day now young enthusiasts set out from Chipping Norton at three o'clock in the morning to see

46

the sun rise directly behind the King Stone as they stand within the circle. Those who prefer to visit the historic circle at a later hour can admire the magnificent view and try to count the stones, for tradition has it that, like Stonehenge, the total will never be the same twice in succession!

The Empress Matilda's Escape

❧

A bitter and cruel civil war ravaged England after the death of Henry I in 1135 and both Oxford and Wallingford were involved in the struggle for power between Henry's daughter, Matilda, and his nephew, Stephen of Blois.

Henry had received assurances from his barons that they would give their allegiance in the succession to Matilda, his only surviving legitimate child, but after his death they began to doubt the wisdom of their promises made to the late king. Henry had kept his powerful barons in check but now, when some of the more unscrupulous lords cast jealous glances at their weaker neighbours' possessions, those who wanted peace and prosperity for England thought a woman would be powerless to control the great landowners.

The merchants of London, whose trade had prospered under a strong king, thought that their future would be more secure with a man upon the throne and so they openly welcomed Stephen when he arrived in London as soon as Henry's death was announced.

But Matilda was not without her influential supporters. Her mother was the daughter of the Scottish king, Malcolm III, and although Malcolm was dead, his son King David, rallied to his niece's cause and came over the Border to ravage the north of England. In the south her half-brother, Robert, Earl of Gloucester, the illegitimate son of Henry, and one of the most powerful barons, proclaimed his support for Matilda.

Matilda was herself all too familiar with court intrigue. She had been married in childhood to the Emperor Henry V of Germany but had returned to England on her husband's death. She was later married to Geoffrey, Count of Anjou, to suit her father's interests, but she retained her title of Empress. Now, as she waited in her husband's domains in France, Stephen's followers seized their opportunity and crowned him King of England.

In the years which followed the land was ravaged by war and evil men fought their own feuds under the cover of the main conflict until all Englishmen cried out that Christ and His saints were asleep.

In 1139 Matilda landed in England and two years later she established her headquarters at Oxford. Stephen brought his army to the city in an effort to destroy her but she took refuge in the great castle which Robert D'Oilly had begun building just seventy years before. It stood formidable on the western outskirts of Oxford, overlooking the marshes and the River Thames. For nearly three months the Empress resisted Stephen's attacks but at length the stores of food became exhausted and she decided to leave her stronghold. Winter held the countryside in an unrelenting grip and both marshes and river were frozen and snowcovered so that the slightest movement of dark figures would have been immediately noticed against the white landscape. However, Matilda's escape was carefully planned.

The sentry was bribed and the Empress and her attendants were clothed in white from head to foot. Silently they slipped from the castle and made their way across the frozen river and to Abingdon. How terrified they must have been as they journeyed through the bitter weather, knowing that capture would mean death, or, alternatively, long, cruel, imprisonment. Leaving Abingdon behind, they pressed on to Wallingford where another great castle stood beside the Thames to give them refuge, and time to replan their campaign.

Matilda in fact eventually won the throne but her reign was short and unsuccessful. Her half-brother the Earl of Gloucester died in 1147 and a year later she had to leave England for Anjou again.

Her son, Henry, was continuing the struggle when fate intervened; Stephen's son, Eustace, died in 1153, leaving Henry the heir. By the Treaty of Wallingford it was agreed that Stephen should retain the crown for his lifetime and that Henry should succeed him. Henry had not long to wait. Stephen died a year later and Henry, now twenty-one years of age, was called to rule over a sadly impoverished kingdom.

Today little remains of either Oxford or Wallingford castles but the ruins are sufficient to show the once mighty strength of the two fortresses which provided vital shelter for a sorely pressed Empress.

The Levellers
at Burford

The tranquillity of Burford, the beautiful country town on the banks of the Windrush, was rudely disturbed on the evening of Sunday, May 13th, 1649, when a contingent of three hundred and fifty soldiers marched into the town.

The men were Levellers, those who felt that they had fought a civil war against the King to obtain a truly democratic and egalitarian government and they were dissatisfied and disappointed with the policies pursued by Cromwell's new Commonwealth parliament.

After a skirmish with Colonel Fairfax's army at Salisbury they had come post haste to Burford where they hoped to enjoy a night's shelter before marching on to Banbury. Both Cromwell and Fairfax, however, were determined to suppress the rebellion before it gathered more support and by relentless pursuit the Levellers were overtaken and surprised as they settled down to rest in Burford. Roused from their sleep they put up little resistance. One of their number was killed near the Crown Inn at the corner of Sheep Street and the others soon capitulated to the superior force. The rebels were quickly marched towards the Parish Church, hustled inside, and heard the key turned in the lock, but in spite of all precautions some managed to escape under cover of darkness.

The Vicar, the Reverend Christopher Glynn, quietly buried the soldier who had fallen in the skirmish and waited to see what the next development would be in the strange drama being enacted in his church.

Events moved rapidly. Cromwell held a court martial and an officer was sent to the church to inform the prisoners that they were under sentence of death. The unfortunate men were then left for four days and nights to meditate upon their likely fate. One man whiled away the time by carving his name 'Antony Sedley' and the word 'prisoner' on the lead of the font. It can be seen to this day.

On the Thursday morning the prisoners were taken to the roof of the church by way of a turret staircase, that is, all but four of them. These were the unfortunate men who had been selected for execution — Cornet Thompson, Corporal Perkins, John Church and Cornet Denne, who was a ringleader of the mutiny. Strangely enough, he was the one whom Cromwell pardoned at the last minute due, it is said, to his penitence. The other three faced a firing squad bravely and died by the church wall which still bears the scars of the bullets fired on that fateful day.

The colleagues of the dead men watched the scene from above in horror then silently returned to the church where they were forced to listen to a long discourse by Cromwell followed by a sermon preached by a weeping and humiliated Cornet Denne.

Eventually the chastened rebels were marched to Devizes where they were held for a time before being allowed to rejoin the ranks of the loyal Commonwealth army.

The townspeople, no doubt shocked and disturbed by the events of that turbulent week, saw tranquillity return to their town and the Vicar performed yet another sad duty. He entered in his parish register 'The three soldiers shot to death in Burford churchyard, buried May 17th'.

May Day and Christmas Customs

❦

Perhaps the most famous of all May Day customs is the one which takes place at Magdalen College, Oxford, when the hymn *Te Deum Patrem colimus* is sung by the choir at dawn from the top of the Great Tower.

In spite of the early hour the street is crowded with spectators who gather to hear the song of praise as it floats over the city in the chill morning breeze. No one knows when the custom began. Its origins are probably older than the mediaeval tower itself for, long before Christianity was brought to this country, the pagan worshippers climbed to high places in order to sing praises to the sun.

Another May Day custom which is thought to pre-date the Christian era is that of carrying a doll in a garland of flowers, a ceremony much favoured by the young girls of many towns and villages, who called from door to door to show their dolls in the hopes of collecting pennies from kind hearted neighbours. This practice was long continued at Aston Tirrold and Aston Upthorpe, two villages high on the Berkshire Downs, but since the boundary changes of 1976 now considered as part of Oxfordshire.

In the excitement of gathering the fresh flowers and arranging them around their favourite dolls, few children gave a thought to 'Flora' the Roman goddess of flowers, whose effigy was probably the first to occupy the place of honour in the garlands.

When Augustine brought Christianity to England in 597,

54

he was advised by Pope Gregory to change, rather than destroy, the prevailing customs of the people, knowing that they would more readily embrace the new religion if they could retain some of their familiar ceremonies.

So, the figure of the Virgin Mary in time replaced that of the heathen goddess, but the years of the Reformation brought about a decline in the homage paid to the Virgin, and, ultimately, the fierce Puritanical denunciation of May Day as an idolatrous festival almost brought an end to all the old customs. Almost, but not quite, for with the restoration to the throne of King Charles II in 1660, the spirit of May Day returned. But, in the renewed celebrations, a doll was used as the centrepiece of the children's floral handiwork.

A similar ceremony to that of the floral garlands is still continued at Charlton-on-Otmoor where, from time immemorial, the children have carried small crosses decorated with flowers around the village, singing their May Day song:

A May garland we have brought you
Before your door we stand
It is but a bit and it smells very sweet
And it came from the Lord's right hand.
Good morning ladies and gentlemen
We wish you a happy day
We've come to show you our May garland
Because it's the first of May.

Until 1962 they, too, called at the houses to collect their pennies, but the following year the procedure was changed and the children now take their decorated crosses into the parish church of St. Mary the Virgin. After the service there is traditional dancing in the village street.

The line in the song 'and it came from the Lord's right hand', indicates that the children's garlanded crosses are linked with the smaller of the two large crosses which once stood on the rood screen of the church.

They, in turn, were reminders of much older customs, the first of which again had its foundations in pagan worship. It is thought that a Celtic spring festival included a procession winding through the village in honour of a mother-goddess. No doubt the villagers hoped that by so honouring her they would reap a good harvest in due season.

This was eventually translated into a Christian festival, the heathen goddess being replaced by the Virgin Mary. Reverence was done to her statue which would have stood above the rood screen to the right of the Crucifix, the figure of St. John being on the left hand side, as was the custom before the Reformation. When it was decreed that all such figures must be removed from the churches in 1548, the church of Charlton-on-Otmoor was forced to comply with the order but it managed to retain its very fine rood screen.

In later years it seems that two crosses were placed upon the screen, the smaller of which was thought to represent the Virgin Mary. It was decorated on May Day with box branches and spring flowers and was carried in procession around the village before being returned to the church.

By the mid-nineteenth century only one cross remained but villagers regarded it as the smaller of the two crosses which apparently had been moved to the central position. An old resident, who died in 1914, had decorated this single cross in her younger days and recalled that the evergreens had been well 'waisted' so that the cross bore resemblance to the figure of a lady when completed. It was carried in procession through the village as late as 1904.

The old custom then fell into disuse but it was revived in 1977 so that the garlanded cross, suitably 'waisted', stands once more on the rood screen of the church of St. Mary the Virgin. The evergreens are renewed in September for Dedication Day, and then remain throughout the winter months to await the fresh branches and spring flowers of May.

The church at Charlton-on-Otmoor is under the patronage of Queen's College, Oxford, where another time honoured custom is still observed, that of garnishing a boar's head for the Christmas feast.

The legend connected with the origin of this custom is stated to have no historical foundation. Never-the-less it is worth recalling, if only as an epic tale of the courage and resourcefulness of a young man faced with imminent danger.

The old story tells of a scholar of Queen's College who was wandering in the woods of Shotover while studying Aristotle. Suddenly, he was confronted with a wild boar but instead of taking to his heels (surely a tempting impulse under such circumstances) he bravely stood his ground and thrust his book into the animal's throat, thereby choking him. The head was carried in triumph to the college dining table.

However that may be, as a boar's head was one of the delicacies of a mediaeval banquet, it was naturally served at a dinner held in honour of the Christmas festival. It was no doubt appreciated by the homesick residents of the College, who were unable to return home because of the hazards of winter travel in the middle ages. Many came from Cumberland and Westmoreland to study at Queen's, which was founded in 1341 by Queen Phillippa's chaplain and confessor, Robert d'Eglesfield, who was himself a native of Cumberland.

Now that distance does not prevent any of the College residents from returning home the ceremony has been brought forward and takes places at the end of the Michaelmas term. The alteration was made in 1961 as the College was almost deserted at Christmas, except for some Fellows in residence, and many graduates left Queen's without ever having seen the famous ceremony.

The boar's head may now be replaced by the less romantic sow's head obtained from a local butcher, but it is still garnished with rosemary and bay and has the traditional orange placed in its mouth. Gilded holly and small hand-painted banners complete the decoration. The head is placed on a silver dish, thoughtfully presented to his old college by Sir Joseph Williamson in the seventeenth century.

Two cooks carry in their masterpiece to the accompaniment of a carol, sung by the boys of Queen's College choir.

The Boar's head in hand bear I
Bedecked with bays and rosemary,
And I pray you my masters be merry,
Quod estis in convivio.

As the singing ends the dish is placed before the Provost who presents the gilded herbs and the orange to the Cantor and his choir.

Even the hazards and the shortages of the second World War could not halt the centuries old custom. A papier mâché head was substituted for the real thing and decorated in the true spirit of resourcefulness, and courage, of the mediaeval Queen's scholar, even if he is lost in the mists of mythology.

Fair Rosamund

⁂

Devout nuns dwelt by the Thames at Godstow for four centuries, but it is not for their piety that the nunnery is remembered but rather for its connection with Fair Rosamund, the beautiful mistress of King Henry II.

Godstow Nunnery was founded by the Benedictines in 1138 and the dedication service was attended by King Stephen and his queen. It was chosen by Walter de Clifford as a place of education for his daughter, Rosamund, and while she was there she came to the notice of the then king, Henry II, probably when he was in residence at his royal palace of Woodstock, some five miles distant from Godstow.

Henry took the young girl to Woodstock where he built her a house. Ruins, thought to be those of this house, stood on the royal estate until the beginning of the eighteenth century, when they were demolished during the building of Blenheim Palace. Now only Rosamund's well remains.

The house was set in a secret place surrounded by a maze so that Rosamund might be hidden from Henry's queen, the formidable Eleanor of Aquitaine, who, with good reason, was jealous of her husband's paramour. Rosamund bore Henry two sons, William Longspee, Earl of Salisbury, whose tomb can be seen in Salisbury Cathedral,and Geoffrey, who eventually became Lord Chancellor of England.

According to legend, Queen Eleanor finally managed to penetrate the maze, which was shaped like a knot, and poison her rival. It was Ranulf Higden, a fourteenth century monk of Chester, who first recorded the story of the maze and the queen's murder of Rosamund, no doubt a tale beloved by the wandering mediaeval minstrels. It was later elaborated by the

59

sixteenth century historian, John Stowe. They contended that Eleanor found her way through the maze by a clue provided by a silken thread, and then forced the distraught girl to drink the poison. Later legends suggest that Rosamund was offered a choice between death by poison or the dagger, and chose the former as being the lesser of two evils. There may be some foundation for these theories, but as Queen Eleanor was extremely unpopular during her lifetime people were only too ready to seize upon stories, true or false, which would discredit her memory. Historians now believe that it was far more likely that Rosamund eventually returned to Godstow and died from natural causes in 1176.

Whatever the reason for her death, King Henry richly endowed the convent and had a magnificent tomb erected over Rosamund's burial place in the choir. It was hung with silken curtains. Devoted nuns kept lamps and candles burning continuously, and prayed for the soul of one who had brought benefactions to their house. Such devotion to the memory of a woman who had been the mistress of a king horrified Bishop Hugh of Lincoln when he visited Godstow in 1191. He ordered the nuns to remove Rosamund's remains from the choir and to place them outside the church. Reluctantly his orders were obeyed but as soon as the Bishop had departed the nuns gathered the scattered bones and placed them in a perfumed leather bag which they laid reverently inside a lead coffin in the Chapter House. There they remained until the mid sixteenth century when the nunnery was dissolved and desecrated by order of King Henry VIII. The antiquarian, John Leland recorded that when the lead coffin was opened 'a very sweet smell came out of it.'

The last Abbess handed over her convent to the King's Commissioners and it passed into the hands of his physician, George Owen. It continued as a private house until the time of the Civil War. At that time it was garrisoned for King Charles I but it was taken in 1646 and almost completely destroyed by order of the Puritan commander, Colonel Fairfax.

Now only a few walls remain to remind us of a young girl who walked in the still peaceful meadows over eight hundred years ago, and captured the heart of a wayward king.

The Profligate Earl

⤜∞⤛

John Wilmot was only ten years of age when he became the 2nd. Earl of Rochester, Baron Wilmot of Adderbury in England and Viscount Wilmot of Athlone in Ireland. His father had died in Bruges, a penniless exile but loyal, as always, to the Stuart cause.

As Henry, Lord Wilmot, he had survived the Civil War and followed the uncrowned king, Charles II, into exile, leaving Lady Wilmot in England to care for their young son, and her two elder sons by a previous marriage. In 1651 he had returned to fight with Charles at the Battle of Worcester and, when all was lost, he shared in the perilous escape of the fugitive king. On a chill October morning they had sailed from Shoreham in the *Surprise* to face further years of exile together.

Apart from his participation in another abortive attempt to overthrow the Commonwealth, which ended with Colonel Penruddock's ill-fated rebellion in 1655, Lord Wilmot, the First Earl of Rochester, as he now was, remained abroad until his death in 1658, two years before the king, whom he had served so faithfully, was finally restored to the throne.

His son, the new young earl was educated at Burford Grammar School, where he proved an apt pupil, and was then sent by his ambitious mother to Wadham College, Oxford, just before he was thirteen years of age. He was created Master of Arts in September, 1661 and at the end of that year began the fashionable Grand Tour of France and Italy.

With the final stage of his education accomplished the Earl returned home in 1664 and made his first appearance at Court, still only seventeen but well versed in the ways of the world and already noted for his wit and audacity, attributes which endeared him to King Charles II, who also welcomed him as the son of his old friend and companion in exile.

However, the favoured young man was soon to incur the King's anger and find himself committed to the Tower of London.

It was all on account of a beautiful heiress, Elizabeth Mallett of Enmore in Somerset. She was being courted by a large number of hopeful suitors under the watchful eyes of her mother and her two guardians, her stepfather, Sir John Warre, and her grandfather, Lord Hawley. Lord Rochester's suit was favoured by the King and his influential mistress Lady Castlemaine, but the young man's fortune was small, a matter which he felt might weigh heavily against him in the deliberations of the two guardians, so that he decided to take matters into his own hands. As Elizabeth Mallett was returning to her home one evening in the company of her grandfather their coach was stopped at Charing Cross by a band of armed men, under the direction of Lord Rochester. The young lady was dragged from the coach and transferred to a waiting vehicle drawn by six horses which sped off along the road westwards. However, pursuit was swift and Rochester was overtaken at Uxbridge although the kidnapped heiress was not found for another day or two. The King was furious at this outrageous behaviour by one of his courtiers and commanded that the Earl should be taken to the Tower. However, he was eventually released after craving the King's pardon, and he then served gallantly with the English fleet against the Dutch navy, after which he was restored to royal favour.

Finally success, and with the King's blessing, Lord Rochester was married to Elizabeth Mallett in January 1667. Early the following month, after a visit to the theatre, Samuel Pepys recorded in his diary, 'Here I saw my Lord Rochester and his lady, Mistress Mallett, who after all this ado married him, but, as I hear some say in the pit, it is a great act of charity for he hath no fortune.'

It was the beginning of a lonely and troubled married life for the heiress who spent most of her time alone at Adderbury, the Oxfordshire manor which had been leased by the Earl's grandfather from the Bishop of Winchester in 1629.

During the Commonwealth period the estate had been sequestrated and sold but at the Restoration it was recovered by the Bishop, and Anne, Lady Rochester, the widow of the first earl, had renewed the lease so that Adderbury was once more the Wilmots' family home. While his wife and mother resided quietly in the country the Earl lived his own profligate life at court, sometimes amusing the King by his witty satirical verses, at other times enraging the monarch when the verses lampooned Charles himself and the royal mistresses.

Occasionally the Earl returned to Oxfordshire and briefly enjoyed the peace of the countryside. At High Lodge in Woodstock, where he resided in his capacity of Ranger of Woodstock Park, he entertained his court cronies, but at Adderbury House he was content with his wife's company and that of his only son, Charles, and his three daughters, Anne, Elizabeth, and Mallett. His wife, apparently always forgiving and pleased to share his company, must have delighted in these short visits when she and her errant husband entertained their few mutual friends.

Unfortunately these periods of happiness were all too rare and the restless earl, still in his twenties, would be off again, leaving his wife and mother to grieve over the wild stories of his wayward behaviour.

One such story alleged that the Earl and his friend, the Duke of Buckingham, being sadly out of favour with the King, left the court and bought a tavern on the Newmarket road. In their new role as landlords they dispensed lavish hospitality, especially to any customers who could be persuaded to bring their pretty wives to the inn. One elderly man of puritanical disposition always came alone, but it was well known that he had a beautiful young wife who was closely guarded by his aged sister whenever he was away from home. That was enough to spur on the reprobate innkeepers and while Buckingham welcomed the old man to the inn the Earl called at his house dressed in woman's clothing. Rumour had told him that the elderly chaperone was fond of her alcohol and he had carefully prepared a drugged cordial before he presented himself on the doorstep. As soon as the door was opened he effectively swooned and was quickly admitted into the house. Remedies were brought to revive the ailing visitor but soon the chaperone was persuaded to steady her own fluttering nerves and she swallowed the prepared cordial. The lovely young wife needed little encouragement to slip away from her dull home and accompany the Earl to the inn, but before she left she took possession of her husband's savings. When the unfortunate man returned home he found his sister sleeping soundly, his wife flown, and his gold missing. It is said that the next morning he was found hanging from a beam, but this did not worry the principal actors in the drama or the man's young widow who was eventually sent on her way to London to find a more amiable husband. The King, on hearing the story, was amused and the two impostors left their tavern to indulge once more in the pleasures of the court, pleasures for which Lord Rochester was to pay dearly.

In his early thirties he was forced to retire to Woodstock, his body wasted by dissipation and his mind troubled as he realised that he had not long to live. His wife and mother came from Adderbury to nurse him and he was attended by eminent doctors and divines, the latter calling upon him to repent of his profligate ways. Strangely enough, he seemed anxious to comply but found it difficult to accept their devout theories. Eventually, it was a country cleric, Robert Parsons, Vicar of Adderbury and chaplain to the Rochester family, who brought about the Earl's conversion and repentance before he died on 26th. July, 1680.

It was to Robert Parsons that the Earl confided that he hoped his young son would never be a wit, a wish which was to be tragically fulfilled as Rochester's wife and son both died a year later. Anne, dowager Lady Rochester, then aged sixty six, saw the title which had been bestowed upon her royalist husband become extinct with the death of her grandson, Charles Wilmot, third and last Earl of Rochester.

Disaster on Christmas Eve

The train from London to Wolverhampton was jolting along at forty miles an hour on Christmas Eve, 1874. It was around noon and the passengers were contemplating a pleasant Christmas holiday and, in many cases, a reunion with their families.

So many people had joined the train at Oxford that an extra coach was found to be necessary, and another engine was also added as two more coaches had been connected at Reading, and judging by the number of seasonal travellers, the Oxford station master considered that other carriages might be needed before the journey ended.

The crowded train continued on its way. As it passed through the tiny village of Hampton Gay, and drew near to Shipton-on-Cherwell station, the driver of the second engine noticed that the rope of the alarm bell was moving. It passed over the tops of the coaches from the rear of the train and should have been connected to the bell but this was not ringing. Someone was obviously trying to attract the driver's attention, without success.

The driver, Henry Richardson, looked back down the train and saw that something was wrong. He shut off steam and blew the brake whistle, but the driver of the first engine had also become alarmed by that time. Both drivers frantically applied their brakes. It was too late. The rear portion of the train had already left the rails.

It travelled three hundred and fifty yards, churned through

the sleepers, across a wooden bridge which spanned the Cherwell, and then crashed down the embankment into the meadows adjoining the Oxford and Birmingham Canal. A wheel-tire had broken on the carriage which had been joined to the train at Oxford.

The proprietor of the Hampton Gay paper mills, Mr. R. Langton Pearson, ran to the scene of the disaster followed by his workmen, and with the aid of those passengers who were unhurt, they managed to extricate the injured from the wreckage, and carry them to the proprietor's home, part of the old Hampton Gay manor house. Others were taken into the mill. Fortunately, Mr. Mallam, an Oxford surgeon was attending a patient at a nearby house and quickly arrived to give help. He was assisted by a young London doctor who was travelling on the train. The bodies of the twenty six dead passengers were carried to the mill.

Some of the carriages were completely wrecked, others had

slipped into the icy waters of the Canal. Snow had been falling and telegraph lines were down, but after some delay messages eventually reached Woodstock and Oxford. Lord Randolph Churchill came from Blenheim Palace, together with ladies from the Duke of Marlborough's family. They brought food and drink for the injured which must have been very welcome on the bitterly cold night.

Nearly an hour had passed before more doctors arrived by special train from Oxford, bringing with them much needed medical supplies. Fifty of the injured were then taken to the Radcliffe Infirmary, the remainder were distributed around Oxford. Christmas preparations were forgotten as they arrived at the doors of the Randolph Hotel, New College, Jones' Railway Hotel, and the King's Arms Hotel, and were carried to the vacant bedrooms. More than seventy passengers had been injured, and over thirty had died, for some of the injured did not survive the rail journey to Oxford. Their bodies were placed in the station waiting room. People of all ages had been involved, and from all walks of life.

Queen Victoria sent messages of sympathy to the bereaved, and made inquiries as to the progress of the injured. The whole nation was stunned by the news of what was then the worst accident ever in railway history.

The few residents of Hampton Gay were obviously in no mood for Christmas festivities, surrounded as they were by evidence of the tragedy, and New Year readers of the *Illustrated London News* were made fully aware of the grim realities by harrowing drawings made by an artist on Christmas Day. He could never have had such a miserable assignment as he had that day.

The Great Western Railway set up an immediate inquiry as to the cause of the accident, and the inquest was opened at Hampton Gay on Boxing Day, and at Oxford the following Monday, by Mr. W. Brunner, the coroner for the city and county of Oxford, but it was March before the verdict was reached.

By that time many statements had been taken, and accusations made; tempers became frayed by the long drawn out proceedings. The delay was mainly due to the slow recovery of some of the injured whose evidence was needed before the verdict could be announced. The conclusion reached by the jury was that it was a pure accident, chiefly due to the prevailing weather conditions which affected the wheel-tire.

However, several recommendations were made regarding the adoption of additional safety precautions, and for improved testing of the communication cords. This point was strongly urged by Lord Randolph Churchill in a letter to *The Times*, together with a demand for a better braking system for all express trains.

Compensation was paid by the railway but that was of little comfort to all who had suffered bereavement on that sad Christmas Eve.

Twelve years after the accident the house to which the injured had been taken was gutted by fire, but Mr. Langton Pearson had already moved away. Perhaps he could not bear the memories of that night, for in all its history the Elizabethan manor house could never have seen such tragedy as on the Christmas Eve of 1874.

Where Goes the Garter?

Two fifteenth century noblewomen of Oxfordshire little thought that their tombstone effigies would one day solve a problem for Queen Victoria.

The first of the noble ladies was born Alice Chaucer, the only child of Thomas and Matilda Chaucer, and a granddaughter of Geoffrey Chaucer, the fourteenth century poet. Alice inherited the manor of Ewelme from her mother and, upon her marriage to John de la Pole, Earl of Suffolk, the rich and powerful minister of King Henry VI, the Suffolk family planned to turn Alice's inheritance into a model mediaeval village.

Their scheme was an ambitious one for that period. It allowed for considerable extensions to the manor house, the rebuilding of the parish church, and the erection of two new establishments, a school for the education of the young, and a group of almshouses for thirteen poor, elderly men. These houses were to be built around a courtyard at the west end of the church, with covered steps leading up to a door so that the residents could conveniently enter the church to pray for their benefactors.

By 1437 the work was sufficiently advanced for two chaplains to be appointed, one as headmaster of the school, the other as master of the almshouses, but the Earl did not live to see the completion of the entire project. In spite of his generous gifts to Ewelme, and his elevation to a dukedom by the King, he was intensely disliked nationally. His rise to power had been by somewhat doubtful ways and he had made many enemies. In 1450 the Duke left England for France and was brutally murdered while crossing the Channel.

The Duchess was left to supervise the work alone and devoted the twenty five years of her widowhood to the welfare of her village. The manor house has disappeared but the church, school, and almshouses still testify to her bounty. If a further reminder is needed of the beneficent Duchess it is provided by her magnificent tomb, erected after her death in 1475, which can be seen in the Church of St. Mary the Virgin.

It is a splendid example of fifteenth century craftsmanship. Underneath, behind delicate arcading lies a sinister reminder that in death all are equal. Usually the symbol of a skull satisfied the mediaeval moralists but here a shrunken corpse of an elderly woman is finely sculptured. It is horrible in its accuracy. However, above the arcading all is beauty and perfection. The effigy of the duchess is carved in finest alabaster, her face is serenely beautiful, a coronet rests lightly over a veiled head-dress, her gown falls in graceful folds around a still youthful figure (she was seventy one when she died), and on her left arm, between the wrist and the elbow, she wears the Order of the Garter.

It is this feature which links the effigy of the Duchess of Suffolk with that of the other mediaeval noblewoman whose effigy lies in the Church of St. Michael at Stanton Harcourt.

There, in the southeast corner of the Harcourt chapel, can be seen the tomb of Sir Robert Harcourt and his wife, Margaret, daughter of Sir John Byron. They, too, were builders, enlarging the manor house, and building a private chapel where their arms can still be seen emblazoned on the walls, although much of the old house has now disappeared.

Sir Robert, the holder of many honours, was created High Steward of the University of Oxford in 1447, and Knight of the Garter in 1464. His wife, too, was thus honoured for both are depicted wearing the Order, he on his left leg as is still the custom, while Lady Margaret wears her Garter on the left arm, but unlike the Duchess of Suffolk, it rests above her elbow.

72

When Queen Victoria ascended the throne and became Sovereign of the Order of the Garter no one was quite sure where a lady should wear the Garter. None of the Hanoverian kings had honoured their consorts by investing them with the noble Order, and it seems that earlier reigning queens had left no record, so it was decided that the tombs of some of the earliest lady recipients must be visited. Perhaps they would show where the symbol of this order of chivalry had been placed?

Only three such tombs were known to exist, the two in Oxfordshire and one in London, where, in the Collegiate Church of St. Katherine, the effigy of Constance, daughter of the Duke of Exeter, was recorded as bearing the Order of the Garter. However, her tomb was so defaced that it was of no help to the Victorian researchers who then travelled to the churches at Ewelme and Stanton Harcourt to find a solution to their problem.

After the two effigies had been carefully studied, approval was given to the positioning of Lady Margaret's Garter, and Queen Victoria was advised to wear the Order above the elbow of her left arm. It is this position which is still favoured by lady Members of his highest order of English knighthood.

Love Poisoned

On an August day in 1751 a terrified woman ran down Hart Street, Henley, toward the river Thames followed by an angry mob. She found brief refuge in the Angel Inn before being arrested and taken to Oxford gaol.

It was the beginning of the end of a tragic drama which had begun on an evening five years before when the town clerk of Henley, Francis Blandy, his wife, and their daughter, Mary, drove happily together to Paradise House to dine with General Mark Kerr.

Mr. Blandy, a successful solicitor, was proud of his only child. She was no great beauty but she had a trim figure, fine dark eyes, and a pleasing disposition, and her father made no secret of the fact that Mary's dowry would be in the region of ten thousand pounds, and that on her parents' death she would inherit a considerable fortune.

However, Mary (or Mollie as she was affectionately called) and her handsome dowry were not to be bestowed lightly, and her watchful father frowned upon any ineligible suitors. Consequently at twenty-six Mary was still unmarried.

Mr. and Mrs. Blandy were gratified, therefore, when that evening General Kerr's cousin, Captain the Honourable William Cranstoun, paid particular attention to their daughter. They were not unduly disturbed that he was forty-six years of age, far from handsome, small in stature, and scarred by smallpox. In spite of these physical drawbacks he had a certain charm of manner, and, most important of all, he was nobly born, being a son of a Scottish peer, William, 5th. Lord Cranstoun. The fact that he was a younger son of an impoverished family did not deter them. In the eyes of Mr.

and Mrs. Blandy his birth alone made him an eligible suitor for their daughter's hand.

The Captain became a frequent visitor to their home in Hart Street. He was stationed in Henley for some time on recruiting duties and being solely dependant upon his pay, and excessively extravagant, he was only too pleased to ingratiate himself into a household which boasted a well endowed single daughter.

Mrs. Blandy in particular was delighted with the way the courtship was proceeding. Her own health was giving cause for concern and she was pleased that her daughter, now deeply infatuated with Cranstoun, was on the way to becoming well established in society.

General Mark Kerr, however, was far from happy when he realised what was happening and eventually he informed Mr. Blandy that his cousin was already married, with a wife and child living in Scotland.

Inquiries soon revealed that Captain Cranstoun was indeed a married man. He had wed Anne Murray in Edinburgh on the 22nd. May, 1744, but as his wife was a Roman Catholic, and a daughter of a Jacobite family, the marriage had been kept secret for fear that the bridegroom's chances of promotion might be affected. When the Captain had been ordered South, his wife had returned to her family home with their small daughter.

The plausible Captain Cranstoun managed to persuade Mr. and Mrs. Blandy, and Mary, that the marriage was over and could easily be annulled by the Scottish courts. He further placated Mary by the gift of a brooch of Scottish pebbles as a token of his love for her.

Mrs. Blandy's death and the Captain's recall to duty in Scotland did nothing to abate Mary's devotion to her lover, but Mr. Blandy became increasingly uneasy about the whole affair, especially when difficulties arose concerning the nullification of the marriage.

At length the anxious father became convinced that he had encouraged a scheming fortune hunter to his house and he forbade Mary to have anything further to do with her once favoured suitor. It was too late, his daughter could not bring herself to dismiss her lover and was in despair about her father's stern disapproval. Cranstoun sent her a packet of white powder, ostensibly to clean the pebbles in her brooch, but, he added, the powder was in fact a love philtre which, if added in small quantities to her father's food, would bring about a change of heart in her forbidding parent's attitude to their courtship.

The poor deluded girl believed him and slowly but surely administered doses of arsenic to her father. As Mr. Blandy lay dying he realised that he had been poisoned but he forgave his daughter and again begged her to give up all thoughts of Cranstoun. The unfortunate Francis Blandy died on August 14th. 1751. Mary, who had been confined to her room on the orders of a suspicious doctor, escaped as her father's body was being examined and rushed from the house towards the river bridge but neighbours followed her in swift pursuit until the landlady of the Angel Inn gave her shelter.

Mary was charged with the murder of her father and was brought to trial on 29th. February, 1752. As the Town Hall in Oxford was being rebuilt the trial took place at the Divinity School, an imposing building in which to fight for one's life. Mary Blandy showed little emotion throughout the proceedings until an old family friend, Mrs. Mountenay, was called to give evidence against her. Then, for a moment or two, her fortitude was shaken but she recovered and listened impassively as the evidence built up against her. To the end she maintained that she was innocent as she had no idea that the powder contained arsenic. Her protestations were in vain, the jury proclaimed her guilty, sentence was passed, and Mary Blandy returned to the gaol to await her execution.

During the following weeks the condemned woman remained perfectly calm and quietly accepted the unusual privileges which were given to her. She had her own rooms in the keeper's house and several friends were allowed to visit her, but at length the fateful day arrived, and having said her prayers, Mary Blandy was hanged on April 6th. 1752.

Her body was taken to Henley and interred at midnight between the coffins of her parents in the chancel of St. Mary's Church. Despite the late hour several local people made their way to the church, not from morbid curiosity, although that may have accounted for a few of the midnight mourners, but mainly because many Henley residents believed Mary Blandy when she pleaded that she was unaware of the poisonous content of the powder.

Captain Cranstoun did not entirely escape retribution. He fled to the Continent and finally reached the Flemish town of Furnes where he died in agony in December, that same year. His fatal illness showed signs of arsenical poisoning.

Although undoubtedly an unscrupulous scoundrel he, too, had been deluded. Sadly, Mr. Blandy's fortune had been much overrated and had the truth been told about Mary's dowry and expectations, she might never have been embroiled in her ill-fated love affair.

The Lovells of Minster

It is uncertain when the Lovell family was granted the picturesque manor of Minster on the banks of the Windrush but it was probably around the year 1124 when William Lupellus, the first of the Lovells, received large grants of land scattered throughout England from Henry I, whose policy it was to so divide the land of his nobles that their power in any one place was strictly limited.

By the end of the thirteenth century the manor was known as Minster Lovell to distinguish it from the neighbouring manor of Little Minster. By this time the Lovells had prospered both in rank and wealth. Fortune continued to favour them throughout the next century so that the seventh baron, William, Lord Lovell, inherited a substantial fortune when his father died in 1414.

After a further inheritance in 1423 it was natural that the wealthy young nobleman wished for a more spacious and comfortable home than the old manor house provided, but fighting in France occupied his time on and off for the next eight years and it is thought that his rebuilding scheme was delayed until after 1431.

Nine years later William Lovell was granted a royal licence by King Henry VI to enclose Minster Wood and two adjoining fields although the area was part of the King's forest of Wychwood. In 1442 he received permission to disafforest Minster Wood and place it under the care of his own keepers to the exclusion of the King's forest officers. To receive grants of land within the royal hunting ground was indeed an indication of how high he stood in the King's favour. It would seem that Lord Lovell had at last achieved his ambition; his fine house was built and, furthermore, surrounded by extensive parkland.

After William's death in 1455 the royal favour was extended to his son John, the eighth baron who was made master forester of Wychwood. John loyally supported King Henry VI and the Lancastrian cause when trouble brewed throughout England and the quarrel between the royal houses of Lancaster and York divided the nobles of the land.

In spite of John's strong Lancastrian loyalties, his son, Francis, who succeeded his father when still a minor, favoured the House of York when he grew to manhood and became a staunch supporter of Richard, Duke of Gloucester. He was well rewarded for this switch of family loyalty. When Richard became king in 1483, after the murder in the Tower of London of his two young nephews, he created Francis the first Viscount Lovell and heaped additional honours upon him. So great was Lovell's power as Constable of Wallingford, Chamberlain of the Household, and Chief Butler of England, that he figured in the contemporary doggerel verse which claimed:

'The catte, the ratte and Lovell the dogge
Rylyth all England under the Hogge'

The catte and the ratte referred to Catesby and Ratcliffe, two other favourites of the king, the dogge to the hound on Lovell's crest and the hogge to the King himself, whose crest carried a wild boar.

The hated rule was destined to be short lived. It ended at the Battle of Bosworth Field in 1485 with the defeat and death of Richard and the crowning of Henry Tudor as King Henry VII of England. Francis Lovell fled to France but he returned two years later to support a rebellion headed by Lambert Simnel, an impostor who was presented by the Tudor kings' opponents as a claimant to the throne.

Henry VII defeated the rebel army at Stoke near Newark,

and once again Lord Lovell was on the losing side. At first it was thought that he had perished in the battle but later it was rumoured that he had galloped from the field and had attempted to swim the river Trent with his horse, only to be drowned before reaching safety. Still later another story was in circulation. This claimed that Lord Lovell had reached the further bank and had then made his way to Minster Lovell to take refuge in a secret room in the house. A faithful servant had held the key and had promised to supply his master with food until he could make good his escape but something had gone wrong with the plan. Lord Lovell was never seen again.

Years afterwards this story had a sequel. In 1708 the foundations for a new chimney were being laid at the Hall when the workmen discovered an underground vault. They forced their way in and briefly saw a skeleton seated at a table with a book, pen and papers before him, and a decaying cap lying on the floor. All too quickly the remains reacted to the sudden influx of fresh air and as the workmen gazed in wonder the grisly spectacle turned to dust.

Whatever the truth of this strange story it is one which may explain the complete disappearance of the ninth and last Lord Lovell. Was the skeleton his, and did the servant betray his master and leave him to starve to death, or did some sudden illness resulting in the death of the servant prevent him from fulfilling his promise to serve Lord Lovell faithfully?

Later restorations have never revealed an underground room of any kind and the ruins of Minster Lovell Hall may never throw further light upon their grim secret but it is pleasant to wander by the cool waters of the Windrush and gaze upon the grey walls which once were the home of the proud mediaeval family. Whatever the merits of its sons as lords of the manor or national statesmen, the Lovells chose a very beautiful place in which to enjoy their leisured and more peaceful hours in a turbulent period of England's history.

Blankets from
Witney

Witney has been the centre of a thriving woollen trade since the middle ages. Two natural factors have contributed to its success, the Cotswold sheep and the River Windrush, which not only provided power for the mills but whose waters proved especially suitable for the scouring of the woollen cloth. However, these attributes would have been wasted had not the townspeople used them well. Today Wintey can be justly proud of its ability to produce world famous blankets.

In the year 1669 Richard Early had no hesitation in apprenticing his fourteen year old son, Thomas, to the woollen trade. It would not only provide him with settled employment but held good prospects for an intelligent, hard-working youth. Even so, Mr. Early could never have foreseen that three hundred years later, and eight generations down the family tree, his son's descendants would still be making blankets in the town of Witney.

Thomas did not disappoint his father. By 1688 he was already a leading master weaver in the town, and was chosen to present a pair of gold fringed blankets to James II. It was the beginning of a long service to royal customers which has continued to this day.

Witney blankets were already being exported in the seventeenth century, and the weavers included Red Indians among their customers. The cloth was dyed red or blue, colours pleasing to the Indians of Virginia and New England who tore off suitable lengths, made two holes for their arms, and wrapped the remainder of the blanket around their bodies. In return for this warm, colourful clothing the Indians brought furs to the English traders.

In 1711 the Witney weavers were granted a charter to establish a Company of Blanket Weavers. The Weavers' Company in London had been founded in the twelfth century so that Witney's charter was long overdue. The reputable weavers of the town welcomed the formation of the new company as it ensured that no substandard goods would leave the district. All weavers in Witney and for twenty miles around were obliged to bring their blankets to the headquarters of the company to be inspected and hallmarked.

Queen Anne appointed a weaver by the name of John White as the first master of the company but when he died soon after his appointment he was succeeded by Thomas Early. He gladly undertook his new responsibilities as he was as keen as anyone that Witney's blankets should be second to none.

Two subsequent masters of the company, John Early and Job Partlett presented blankets, on behalf of the Witney blanket weavers, to George III and Queen Charlotte, during a royal visit to Nuneham Courtney as guests of Lord Harcourt in 1788.

By that time the invention of new machinery was heralding changes at Witney as in all the manufacturing towns of Britain. The workers grew apprehensive as they saw the machines going into the mills. Anxiety regarding the obvious unemployment they would cause made the men desperate, and they not only sabotaged the machines but, in extreme cases, threatened the very lives of their employers.

The riots developed both in town and country areas as the agricultural workers were equally affected, but progress could not be halted. It soon became evident that machinery had come to stay, although the waters of the Windrush turned the mills themselves until 1837 when steam at last superseded this centuries old method of obtaining power.

The Great Exhibition of 1851 gave English manufacturers

and craftsmen an opportunity to display their skill to the world. John Early showed a patterned blanket, measuring fifty six by seventy five inches, which won him a bronze medallion and a certificate signed by Prince Albert.

There was, however, another exhibit there which caused considerable interest. It had been made forty years before the exhibition when John Coxeter, a woollen merchant of Newbury, was so proud of the new machinery which he had installed in his mill that he boasted that he could take a coat from a man's back, reduce it to wool, and make it into a coat again all within the space of twenty four hours. He was not called upon to honour that commitment, but he was approached by Sir John Throckmorton of Buckland who asked if he could take the wool growing on a sheep's back at sunrise, and make it into a coat by the time of sunset on the same day. Sir John was willing to wager a thousand guineas on the project, and John Coxeter told him to place the wager as he would make the coat in the allotted time. He was as good as his word.

On the morning of June 25th. 1811, Frances Druett, Sir John's shepherd, sheared two Southdown sheep as the sun rose at 5 a.m. Eleven hours later the dyed cloth was ready to be cut out by James White, the son of a Newbury tailor. Nine men were waiting with needles threaded and by twenty minutes past six the coat was finished. There was still one hour and forty minutes before the sun was due to set on that summer's day. That evening Sir John Throckmorton dined with forty friends at the Pelican Inn at Speenhamland, wearing his fine new coat.

No doubt John Early saw the coat at the Exhibition and thought deeply about the record it had created in its day, but it was not until 1906 that Earlys of Wintey challenged the time of eleven hours for the making of the woollen cloth.

On 8th. June, 1906, sheep were shorn at sunrise, and ten hours twenty seven minutes later the blankets were completed, embroidered with a ducal coronet and the letter M, and presented to the Duke of Marlborough. John Coxeter's long standing record had been broken but it had stood for nearly a century, during which time machinery had been vastly improved.

In 1960 the two leading blanket manufacturers of Witney, Earlys and Marriotts, amalgamated, thus strengthening the ties which had been made in the past by intermarriage between the two families.

The company looked forward to the tercentenary of Thomas Early's apprenticeship and the occasion seemed an appropriate time to challenge its own record created at the beginning of the century. So, on June 11th. 1969, one hundred and fifty Kerry Hill sheep were brought to the mill from a Cotswold farm and sheared at 4 a.m. The wool passed through all the necessary processes in record time and the first blanket was ready at 12.11 p.m., eight hours eleven minutes after the shearing.

Before evening fifty blankets had been completed, one of which was flown to New York in time to be displayed with the notice 'The wool of which this blanket is made was shorn from sheep at Witney, England, early this morning.'

The ghosts of Sir John Throckmorton and his friends must surely have drunk a toast that night to 'Earlys of Witney' on the site of the Pelican Inn at Speenhamland.

A Lucky Escape

Chastleton House, which stands five miles northwest of Chipping Norton, was built by Walter Jones, a wealthy woollen merchant of Witney, between the years 1603 and 1618. It is not only owned by his descendants today, but it has remained virtually unchanged since the time when it was planned by its first proud owner.

The old Jacobean house has witnessed the changing fortunes of the family through nearly four centuries but one of its most exciting nights occurred during the ownership of Henry Jones, whose son, Arthur, fought for the Royalist cause at the ill-fated Battle of Worcester in 1651.

As Charles II and his followers left the field in disarray they were relentlessly pursued by the soldiers of the Commonwealth army for Oliver Cromwell had offered a reward of a thousand pounds for the capture of Charles Stuart and every Roundhead hoped to seize the fugitive king. Those Royalists who were fortunate enough to escape the net made their way to their homes and Arthur Jones rode fast to Chastleton.

His relief was immense when he at last entered the gates of his home, stabled his tired horse, and was welcomed into the house by his relieved and thankful wife, Sarah. She hurriedly prepared a much needed meal but she had scarcely placed it before him when the sound of horses' hoofs attracted their attention. Arthur Jones realised that he had been followed and hurriedly made his way to a room over the parlour where rich tapestries concealed the entrance to a secret apartment. As he

86

stepped into his hiding place the knocking at the front door became more persistent and Sarah ran to open it. A party of soldiers stood in the forecourt and their leader demanded to see the Cavalier whose hard ridden horse rested in the stables. Apparently they thought to find the king, but failing that prize they would be satisfied if they captured Arthur Jones who was well known for his Royalist sympathies.

Sarah bravely denied all knowledge of any fugitive and invited them to search the house and outbuildings, but they were tired and hungry after the long pursuit and, confident that they had neatly cornered their quarry, they decided to postpone the search until daylight. They demanded food and a night's resting place from the worried but outwardly calm housewife who obediently brought their supper into the great hall. Presently the unwanted guests mounted the stairs and, of all places, chose to sleep in the room over the parlour. Terrified that they would move the tapestries in the morning and discover the entrance to the secret room, Sarah Jones decided that she must act quickly if her husband was to escape from his now beleagured hiding place.

The good woman prepared a large jug of ale, laced it with laudanum, and took it to the soldiers as a nightcap. They drank the ale gratefully and settled down to rest. Sarah listened outside their door and soon the heavy breathing assured her that her plan had succeeded. She stealthily entered the room, crossed to the secret panel, released it, and so freed her husband. He quickly made his way to the stables, left his own tired mount, and saddled the best of the soldiers' horses to ride away to another secret place.

The estate was heavily fined for the part which Arthur Jones had played at Worcester, and for his subsequent escape, but after two years in hiding he was able to return home and live quietly until the Restoration in 1660. He then planted an oak tree in the grounds of Chastleton House to commemorate a night which would be long remembered in the family's history.

Tales of the Highway

❧

Highway robbery has been glamorised by tales of Robin Hood and similar heroes who robbed the rich to feed the poor, but, more often than not, the 'gentlemen of the road' were nothing more than common muggers whose simple aim was to fill their own capacious pockets. Some had a veneer of breeding and education and were cunning, resourceful men who could blend into a respectable neighbourhood, living a remarkable double life.

Mr. Freeman of Swinbrook was just such a man. At first the local residents were delighted to welcome him as the tenant of the manor house, which for three centuries had been the home of the powerful Fettiplace family.

With the death of the last male heir, George Fettiplace, in 1806, the estate had passed to his five sisters, none of whom wished to occupy the manor, and they were pleased to let it to a wealthy gentleman from London. Mr. Freeman appeared to be a worthy tenant for the ancestral home. He entertained lavishly and invitations to his excellent parties were eagerly awaited, and gladly accepted by the neighbouring gentry.

In return, Mr. Freeman was a welcome guest at any house. His impeccable manners, and charming compliments, endeared him to the ladies while the gentlemen found him an attentive and sympathetic listener, not least when they spoke of the highway robberies which were causing such anxiety in the district.

The immediate area around Swinbrook seemed to escape

the attentions of the robbers but the Gloucester, Banbury, and Worcester roads were not safe to travel. At times it was a lone highwayman who would attack the unwary traveller, but as many as four ruffians had been known to waylay a coach to rob the passengers, once or twice those returning from parties at the manor house. It was all very disturbing and it became obvious that extra precautions must be taken if journeys were to be safely accomplished.

But then one night a coach came under attack which was well guarded and a shot was fired at the highwayman who was wounded and captured. The passengers of the coach recognised him as Mr. Freeman's butler. The Bow Street runners were informed and were the next visitors to the manor house!

Mr. Freeman and his staff were arrested and, when taken to London, they were identified as a much wanted gang of highwaymen. The charming tenant of Swinbrook ended his career on the gallows of Tyburn.

This was the ignominious fate of most highwaymen. Even the renowned Dick Turpin, Claude Duval and Thomas Boulter ended their lives on the gallows, and bodies of less romantic rogues swung from gibbets erected on the highways to serve as grim warnings to those who might be attracted to such a livelihood.

Few men cared to travel after dusk in the eighteenth and early nineteenth centuries when the coaching era was at its peak. But many did, and arrived at their destinations bemoaning the loss of their money and jewellery. Some occasionally had the temerity to withstand the demands of the highwaymen and were successful in bringing the rogues to justice

In 1773 a post-chaise was stopped between Faringdon and Abingdon, then in the county of Berkshire. The highwayman robbed two of the travellers, relieving one of his watch and the other of his money but found that he had met his match with the third passenger who told him to shoot away as he was not going to deliver any of his valuables.

The highwayman was evidently unnerved by this

courageous stand for, after a brief hesitation, he galloped away. The three passengers, elated by the rout of their enemy, mounted the chaise horses to go in pursuit of the robber. They caught their man who was taken before the magistrate, John Elwes, and committed to Reading gaol.

It was found that the highwayman had robbed another post-chaise at Benson a few days before and was awaiting the night coach from Cirencester when the post chaise had come into view and had tempted him into making a rash decision. The thought that here was a bonus hold-up while he awaited his intended victims cost the robber his freedom, and, almost certainly, his life.

However, there was always the risk that the highwayman might accept an invitation to 'shoot away' at its face value.

Mr. Blewitt was the son of an Abingdon coachmaster and was riding to Oxford, where he had business transactions to settle, on January 4th. 1783. He passed the turning to Sunningwell village and soon reached the outskirts of Bagley Wood. The lone horseman looked around as he passed under the overhanging boughs. He had courage but danger lurked behind any tree which was large enough to give cover to a man, and the shadows of Coalpit Bottom were enough to deter the bravest of travellers. His worst fears were then realised, for two men emerged from the wood and demanded that he deliver his money to them at once or they would shoot him dead. Mr. Blewitt didn't think twice. He clapped his spurs to his horse and shouted to them to shoot away. They did, and one bullet passed clean through the brim of his hat as he left them behind.

He reached Oxford safely and his return journey passed without further mishap but undoubtedly the coachmaster's son was relieved and thankful to be safely home in Abingdon that night. His damaged hat must have been examined with interest and wonder by his family and friends as he related the story of his lucky escape in Bagley Woods.

Binsey's Treacle Well

∿

A traveller who turns from the busy Botley to Oxford road as it approaches the city and follows the sign to Binsey finds himself in a completely different environment within a space of a few minutes. The traffic is left behind and peaceful meadows stretch down to the banks of the Thames.

An ancient church, the thatched inn, a farm, and a cluster of houses make up the village of Binsey but throughout the centuries pilgrims have made their way from Oxford, or come by the river, to this secluded place because, in the corner of the churchyard, there is a well — a 'treacle' well, treacle in the mediaeval sense, meaning a healing fluid.

The legend tells us that the well was called forth in the eighth century by St. Margaret in answer to prayers from St. Frideswide who needed healing water to restore the sight of Aelfgar, King of Mercia. It was indeed a generous act on the part of Frideswide as she had been forced to flee from her convent at Oxford to escape the unwelcome attentions of the King. As he pursued her into the forest he was struck by sudden blindness, but far from taking advantage of his plight to further her escape, the saint apparently stayed to help him. Her charitable act appears to have both healed and converted her unwanted lover for he molested her no more. Aelfgar became a Christian and Frideswide returned to her convent to spend her remaining years in peace. She reputedly built a chapel by the well, the forerunner of the present parish church.

The story may have become confused over the centuries but St. Frideswide is still honoured as the patron saint of Christ Church Cathedral, Oxford, where the remains of her shrine can be seen, and the water from St. Margaret's well at Binsey has been sought by countless pilgrims as a cure for eye complaints and other bodily disorders.

In the last century the well was difficult to locate as earth and tangled undergrowth had choked up the spring which feeds it. In fact a visitor to Binsey in the 1850s recorded that the spring was lost and the neighbouring peasantry knew nothing of the well. Fortunately this situation was remedied by the Vicar, the Reverend Thomas Prout, a Christ Church don, who rediscovered the spring in 1857 and fully restored the well in 1874. A protective archway was built, and suitably inscribed, and stone steps gave access to the water so that pilgrims could once again seek the healing qualities of St. Margaret's well, but Oxford undergraduates could not resist the temptation to send gullible tourists in search of Binsey's treacle well, and treacle mines. The two must not be confused according to the older residents of the village for whereas the 'treacle' well is the healing well, the 'treacle mines' were a different proposition. They were shallow ponds, covered in summer with a thick yellow slime which resembled nice sticky treacle.

The tourists were not the only people who were fascinated by stories of the treacle well. As the Reverend Charles Lutwidge Dodgson and his friend, Robinson Duckworth, rowed towards Godstow on a Friday afternoon in July, 1862, they passed by Binsey. Their three guests, Lorina, Alice, and Edith Liddell, the daughters of the Dean of Christchurch asked, as usual, for a story, for they delighted in the fantastic tales which Charles Dodgson related to them. So, the adventures of Alice began, and the dormouse, at the Mad Hatter's tea party, told of the three children, Elsie, Lacie, and Tillie, who lived at the bottom of the treacle well.

The Reverend Charles Dodgson, or Lewis Carroll as he is better known, was persuaded to write down his story, and later to publish it and Binsey's well was thus destined to find further fame through the pages of *Alice in Wonderland*, a far cry from the story of its original healing properties when the clear spring water cured the affliction of an Anglo Saxon king. king.